THE STORY OF ANGLICAN MINISTRY

The Story of Anglican Ministry

by

Edward P. Echlin

 St Paul Publications

ST PAUL PUBLICATIONS
SLOUGH   SL3 6BT   ENGLAND

Copyright © St Paul Publications 1974

Printed in Great Britain by the Society of St Paul, Slough
SBN 85439 102 9

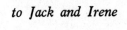

to Jack and Irene

CONTENTS

Preface

Some years ago I concluded a book on the Anglican Eucharist by adding to the dedication page the invocation '*ut mox unum sint*' — that they soon may be one. In the intervening years organic reunion between Canterbury and Rome has become a real, even imminent reality as our two traditions realize that in our disunity we have strayed a space from home.

Since *The Anglican Eucharist in Ecumenical Perspective* appeared I have been asked, on numerous occasions, to prepare a story or narrative of the Anglican Ordinal and Anglican ministry. The story did indeed deserve telling but first it seemed necessary to await a time when the story could have a happy ending.

I believe the time has come — and in this book is the story of Anglican ministry from the Sarum rite which the Edwardine Ordinal replaced to the recent Agreed Statements on eucharist and ministry by the international Anglican/Roman Catholic commission. The story of course will never *really* end until Christian ministry itself enters the parousia. For the distinctive patrimony of Anglicanism will always enhance the one Church of Christ.

As these pages go to press both churches are discerning and evaluating the agreed statements of the international commission. The moment is not yet ripe for Rome publicly to recognize Anglican ministry. But that moment is not far off — and it is our hope that this book will contribute to the event.

An author generally pens a preface after the conclusion of his book. The reader reads just the other way around. That both ending and beginning may be prayerful it is fitting again to end with a prayer in which I hope the reader who is beginning will join — *ut mox unum sint*.

I am grateful to the publishers and to other theologians, both Roman Catholic and Anglican, for their assistance in the preparation of this book. I am especially grateful to the faculties and students at Ushaw College and Lincoln Theological College for their assistance, encouragement and, at times, constructive criticism. I should add that where I have questioned the continuing cogency of Rome's rejection of Anglican ministry and advocated recognition the proposals are my own and are not an attempt to pre-judge the future attitude of my Church. Finally I wish to thank Barbara Larkin for her skillful preparation of the manuscript and all those who in and about Woodsgate and 'the Wendy House', with splendid Anglican hospitality, made a traveller from the colonies very much at home.

Lincoln, England.   Edward P. Echlin
1974

CHAPTER I

The Sarum Background

'And therefore to the entent these orders shoulde bee
continued, and reverentlye used, and estemed in this Church
of England, it is requysite, that no man (not beynge at thys
presente Bisshop, Priest, nor Deacon) shall execute anye
of them excepte he be called, tryed, examined, and admitted,
accordynge to the forme hereafter folowinge.'

The Preface of the Anglican Ordinal, 1550

So read the Preface to a new English Ordinal in the masterful
prose of Thomas Cranmer. The promulgation of the new Ordinal
was a momentous and fateful event in the series of liturgical
changes that ensued upon the death of Henry VIII in 1547. [1]
As early as 1548 Thomas Cranmer, the archbishop of Canterbury,
with the authorization of Parliament had inserted a vernacular
order of communion into the Latin Mass. This vernacular
insertion prescribed communion under both species — and it
was a sign of more radical changes to come. In 1549 a whole
new Communion Service, once again primarily the work of

---

[1] *Concilia Magnae Britanniae et Hiberniae*, David Wilkins, ed., 4 Vols.,
Bruxelles, 1964, Vol. IV, p. 11; *The Order of the Communion 1548*,
H.A. Wilson, ed., 'Henry Bradshaw Society', Vol. XXXIV, London,
1908, no pagination; cf. Edward P. Echlin, *The Anglican Eucharist in
Ecumenical Perspective, Doctrine and Rite from Cranmer to Seabury*,
N.Y., 1968, pp. 22-24.

Cranmer, [2] was established by law as the 'one use' for the whole realm. [3] The eucharist and the church's ministry are so intimately conjoined that it is not surprising that early in 1550, amidst widespread ferment about the faith in eucharist and ministry, Parliament commissioned twelve men to produce a new Ordinal, the legality of which was authorized in advance. [4]

A carefully prepared and radically revised rite for the ordering of deacons, priests and bishops in English lands was immediately submitted to this commission. One Catholic minded member, Bishop Heath of Worcester, was in trouble with the majority only six days after the commission's appointment for his dissenting vote on the new rite which was submitted to the commission as a *fait accompli* and which once again was the work of Thomas Cranmer with some assistance from Bishop Nicholas Ridley and the former Austin Canon Peter Martyr. The new Ordinal in Cranmer's skilful liturgical prose resembles in many respects the Roman pontificals then in use but in its omissions and additions betrays the influence of a draft Ordinal submitted to Cranmer by the Strasbourg reformer Martin Bucer. [5]

From the first meetings of the Ordinal commission in 1550 down to the present moment there has been disagreement and debate about just what Cranmer intended to accomplish with his new rite. Some apologists have argued that he was mainly

---

2 'The First Act of Uniformity', in *Documents Illustrative of English Church History*, H. Gee & W. Hardy, eds., London, 1896, p. 358; Francis Clark, *Eucharistic Sacrifice and the Reformation*, London, 1960, p. 181; C.W. Dugmore, 'The First Ten Years 1549-1559', in The Archbishop of Canterbury et al, *The English Prayer Book, 1549-1662*, London, 1963, p. 9.

3 The First Act of Uniformity, *Documents Illustrative*, Gee & Hardy, eds., pp. 35-81.

4 Francis Procter and Walter Frere, *A New History of the Book of Common Prayer*, London, 1961, pp. 60-61.

5 Martin Bucer, 'De Ordinatione Legitima Ministrorum Ecclesiae Revocanda', in *Scripta Anglicana*, Basle, 1577, pp. 159-186; E.C. Ratcliff, 'The Liturgical Work of Archbishop Cranmer', *Journal of Ecclesiastical History*, October, 1956, p. 201; Constantine Hopf, *Martin Bucer and the English Reformation*, London, 1956, pp. 88-93.

concerned with removing accretions and revising the services according to the primitive ordination rites which were available in the sixteenth century. Others have argued that Cranmer was reacting against the abuses of the contemporary mass system, popular superstition about priest and eucharist, and the defects of late medieval theology. Still others have contended that in the new Ordinal Cranmer was attempting to signify a radical break with the traditional Catholic belief in the Mass as a propitiatory sacrifice presided over by the priest for both living and dead. [6]

There is a good amount of truth in all these arguments. Cranmer was well aware that *lex orandi est lex credendi*. He departed, more by omissions than by additions, from the Roman rite — the Sarum (Salisbury) use being the most common in contemporary England. The Sarum rite incorporates features of the third century *Apostolic Tradition* of Hippolytus, of the later Roman and Gallican sacramentaries, and of additions added in the middle ages. [8] The Sarum rite which Cranmer modified did include and, at least in some parts, stressed a sacrificial emphasis on priesthood in which Cranmer, at least since 1548, no longer believed and which he wanted expunged from both the Communion Service and the Ordinal.

It is sometimes overlooked — and should be noticed here — that the symbolism of sacrificial priesthood gradually developed in the traditional pontifical as the Christian people deepened their understanding of the eucharist as sacrificial and their ministers as priests. The priesthood of bishops and priests *was*

---

[6] There is no need to reprint the bibliography of this centuries' old debate. The traditional arguments are exhaustively discussed and bibliographies provided by two contemporary authors: Francis Clark, *Anglican Orders and Defect of Intention,* London, 1956, and *Eucharistic Sacrifice and the Reformation,* London, 1968, *Stewards of the Lord,* London, 1970; J.J. Hughes, *Absolutely Null and Utterly Void,* London, 1968.

[7] Not in the original Pauline sense that the law of prayer reflected belief in God's *grace* but in the traditional Roman Catholic and Anglican sense that the liturgy reflects belief and vice versa.

[8] David N. Power, *Ministers of Christ and His Church,* London, 1969, pp. 30-95.

B

mentioned as early as the *Apostolic Tradition* which reflects
popular belief stretching back into the second century. The
eucharistic role of ministers was mentioned and signified, but
it was not emphasized. [9] After abatement of the imperial perse-
cutions and the acceptance of clerics as dignitaries and, somewhat
later, with the medieval emphasis on the relation of clerics to
the eucharist, analogies with Old Testament levitical priesthood
and other rites and prayers signifying sacrifice were incorporated
into the ordination rites. The bishops as successors of the
apostles, the role of the hierarchy as pastors and teachers,
especially through holiness of life — these dimensions of ministry
were still reflected in the liturgy, especially in the consecration
rite for bishops. The late medieval pontifical still signified a
comprehensive belief in priesthood. But there was also a new
albeit not exclusive emphasis on sacrifice. Cranmer was keenly
aware, as few reformers before or since have been aware, of the
intimate dialogue and dialectic between faith and this liturgy.
What God's people believe is sooner or later reflected in their
public prayers; what the liturgy teaches in its turn influences
belief. [10] Cranmer was conscious of this principle — and he
therefore produced an Ordinal which signified the new *reformed*
faith in justification, the eucharist and the ministry which was
intended to influence the belief of the people.

Before we can understand Cranmer's novel and brief Ordinal
it is necessary to discuss not only his own belief in the ministry
but the contemporary (and traditional) doctrine which he was
repudiating. It is my conviction that the mainstream of Catholic
doctrine on the ministry, the doctrine which Cranmer was
rejecting along with its many abuses, is clearly reflected in two
sources: in the Roman rite then in use, including its medieval
additions, and in the writings of Stephen Gardiner, the leader
of the Henrician Catholic faction at the time of Cranmer's
liturgical innovations. It is in these two *loci*, more than in the

---

[9] *La Tradition Apostolique de Saint Hippolyte, Essai de Reconsti-
tution*, B. Botte, ed., Munster, 1963; *The Treatise on the Apostolic
Tradition of Saint Hippolytus of Rome*, G. Dix, ed., London, 1968
(2nd ed.).

[10] Barry Till, *The Churches Search for Unity*, London, 1972, pp.
495-502.

rarefied debates of the medieval scholastics or even in the teaching of Trent (which was not primarily concerned with England and which, at any rate, was subsequent to Cranmer's liturgical projects) that the refined belief of Cranmer's English contemporaries may be found. In this chapter we shall concentrate on the Sarum pontifical; thereafter we shall turn to the theology of Gardiner and of Cranmer.

But first an important caution. The Roman rite, including its Sarum version, was, even with the additions inserted in the middle ages, basically a comprehensive rite which signified a comprehensive belief in the meaning of Christian ministry. The Sarum Ordinal which reflected and influenced belief for centuries was — and is — substantially a balanced rite. Cranmer vigourously rejected one aspect of the balance and, therefore, in his own Ordinal deleted sacrificial symbolism. [11] Some reform was indeed desirable and, except for the absence of references to the priest's role at the *sacrificial* memorial in which the living Christ was really present, Cranmer's own Ordinal was itself comprehensive. But the reformers overreacted and that is the tragedy of the reformation. A word of caution is necessary at this point because in the pages that follow we shall especially attend to those parts of the pontifical which signified sacrificial priesthood. In following this method we risk giving the impression that the pontifical taught and conveyed a ministry which was almost exclusively cultic and sacrificial. The fact is that it did not. One may even argue that if anything is emphasized it is the necessary *holiness* in the minister who must lead, teach and sanctify his people. This had been emphasized in the ordination rites, in both East and West, since early patristic times. To mitigate the danger of conveying the impression that the rite almost exclusively signified cultic priesthood we shall in passing mention other features which are included. [12]

---

[11] For some wise remarks on the nature of liturgical language cf. *The Ordination Prayers of the Ancient Western Church,* H.B. Porter, ed., London, 1967, p. xv.

[12] A good example of how a distorted view of Catholic belief in priesthood can devolve from isolating those parts of the pontifical that emphasize sacrifice may be found in Philip E. Hughes, *Theology*

At this point of our study we are concerned with the Sarum pontifical because, according to the true principle that liturgy and belief interreact upon and reflect each other, the ordination rites reflected the centuries' old belief of the church in its ministry.

The Sarum Ordination Rite [13]

The Sarum ordination rite for priests included an optional exhortation or 'admonition' to the ordinands by the ordaining bishop. This custom of instructing ordinands dated back at least to the time of Bishop William Durand in the 13th century. The Sarum admonition began by comparing priests to the sons of Aaron and the bishop to Aaron. This analogy had been popular since the 5th century; originally it signified the bishop's need of assistants, the close association between bishop and presbyters, and God's providence in providing a hierarchy of ministers. In medieval treatises, however, the cultic aspects had been emphasized and this was probably the symbolism read into the Sarum rite in the late middle ages according to the dialogue between belief and liturgy to which we have referred. In the Sarum use the bishop instructs the ordinands that,

> 'in the seventh place was the order of presbyters which in the Old Testament takes its beginning from the sons of Aaron. Those who were then called priests, now presbyters, and who were then called high priests are now called bishops.'

Immediately thereafter the bishop exhorts the ordinands to holiness of life. The presbyter is to be an elder in virtue and

---

of the English Reformers, Grand Rapids, 1965, p. 161. A careful study of the ordination rite *as a whole* reveals a much more comprehensive concept of Catholic ministry. A thorough study of the belief reflected in the Sarum Pontifical would not lead to statements such as the following by G.D.H. Lampe, 'If he [the Anglican priest] is loyal to the Ordinal he cannot, however, rightly claim that he has been ordained to do what the Sarum Pontifical understood to be the principal function of a priest. On the contrary he will be thankful that he has not', in *The Churchman, A Quarterly Review of Anglican Theology,* March, 1962, p. 30.

[13] All references to the Sarum Pontifical will be taken from *Monumenta Ritualia Ecclesiae Anglicanae,* William Maskell, ed., 3 Vols., Oxford, 1882, Vol. II.

holiness as well as in age. Then the admonition enumerates the functions which the presbyter shares with the bishop. The priest's role at the eucharist is not emphasized but it *is* clearly mentioned, thereby reflecting the church's belief in the priest's 'power' to celebrate Mass and to change the elements into Christ's body and blood.

> 'In the other sacraments [i.e. in rites not limited to the episcopal order] whether of catechizing, of baptizing, of celebrating mass, of changing the bread and wine into the Body and blood of Christ, or of preaching in church, the dispensation is shared by both orders.'

It is then stated that priests share all sacramental functions with the bishop (whom they also obey) up to and excluding the conferral of orders. Presbyters are compared to the seventy disciples of the Lord. This analogy emphasizes the priest's prophetic or teaching role. They are also typified in the elders who assisted Moses, the most venerable of the three types of New Testament priesthood referred to in the exhortation. The analogy with the Mosaic elders, which may be found as early as the *Apostolic Tradition,* clearly symbolizes the priest's role as leader.

> Both bishops and priests represent Christ. They call men to penance and they heal them with their prayers. Priests are mediators between God and men.

> 'As good mediators between God and men they convey the precepts of God to the people by preaching the truth, and they offer the prayers of the people to God by interceding for sinners.'

Then the admonition returns to the theme of priestly holiness and refers to the admonitions in the Pastoral epistles about the virtues to be sought in presbyters. At this point the bishop explains one of the later additions to the subsequent ordination rite, the unction of the presbyters' hands. This practice probably originated in the British isles and originally signified sanctification. Later however, when the hands of a presbyter were anointed, unction also connoted the power of consecration. [14]

---

[14] Jasper Ridley, *Thomas Cranmer,* Oxford, 1963, p. 392.

'The hands of the presbyters are anointed just as are the
bishops' that they might know they are receiving in this
sacrament the grace of consecrating so that they should do
works of mercy for all men.'

The bishop explained another late addition to the rite, the
vesting with the stole; here the emphasis is not cultic but on
the virtue expected from a priest. There was another medieval
addition, however, the *porrectio instrumentorum*, or giving of
the paten and chalice to the newly ordained. In both word and
deed this ceremony clearly symbolized the priest's power to
consecrate and offer at the eucharist and this is clearly expressed
in the Sarum admonition.

'They also receive the chalice with wine and the paten
with hosts from the hand of the bishop so that by these
instruments they may know they have received the power
of offering hosts pleasing to God. For it pertains to them
to confect the sacrament of the body and blood of Christ
on the altar, to say prayers, and to bless the gifts of God.'

The sacrificial symbolism of this preliminary part of the
ordination ceremony is further emphasized when, in the admonition, the bishop refers to the priesthood of Christ at the Last
Supper and on the cross. Daily at the altar the priest celebrates
the passion of Christ and reconciles repentant sinners to
God.

'In which it appears how great is the excellence of the
sacerdotal office, through which daily on the altar the
passion of Christ is celebrated and the sinner, converted
from his sins, is reconciled to God.'

The admonition concludes as it began with an exhortation to
holiness on the part of priests that through word and example
they might lead their people to heavenly rewards.

Preceding the ordination service itself there was in the
Sarum rite an unusual rubric, also found in the pontifical of
Archbishop Bainbridge, referring to the integrity of the ordinands' hands. This was omitted by Cranmer. We mention it
here because the special mention of the ordinand's hands
probably refers to the eucharist.

> 'Care should be taken about any mutilation of the body, especially of the hands, which they should show to the bishop.' [15]

The service then begins with an explanation by the bishop of the importance of the priest's function of consecrating and offering at the eucharist — even to the extent of a verbal redundancy. But here again we should observe that this was not the *only* function of the priest which is reflected in the Sarum rite. The redundant addition of 'confect' was not included in some medieval pontificals. [16]

> 'It behooves the priest (*sacerdotem*) to offer, bless, preside, preach, confect, and baptize.'

There immediately followed the solemn and hallowed imposition of hands by the presiding bishop and the presbyters present at the ceremony. This was succeeded by a bidding that all present should pray for heavenly gifts and divine aid for the ordinands. Another prayer invoked the power of the Holy Spirit on these ordinands. Unlike the Exeter and Winchester pontificals Sarum makes no precise mention of 'sacerdotal' grace at this point. [17]

The Sarum preface followed the ancient Verona Sacramentary in referring to the levitical priesthood as part of God's providence. Bishops needed helpers 'of lesser rank'. These assistants made the bishop or 'high priest' present to all his people.

> 'And so the priestly orders and the functions of the levites, established with symbolical rites, increased, when thou didst choose men of lesser degree and lower rank to be the associates and helpers of the high priests whom thou didst appoint to rule the people.'

---

[15] *Ibid.*, p. 213, note 71.

[16] This entire sentence which, in the context of the subsequent ceremony, is redundant does not seem to have been used in the Lanalet Pontifical which was in use for a time at St Germans, Cornwall. Cf. *Pontificale Lanaletense*, G.H. Doble, ed., London, 1937, (Henry Bradshaw Society), pp. 55-57.

[17] *Monumenta Ritualia*, p. 217, note 80.

The preface also recalls the analogy with the seventy elders who assisted Moses in leading God's chosen people and thereby signifies the priest's role as leader of the people. A second analogy, with the seventy two assistants of the apostles, signified the priest's function as preacher. Sarum also compares the priests of the new dispensation to the sons of Aaron.

> 'So too thou didst richly endow the sons of Aaron, Eleazar and Ithamar, from their fathers plenty, in order that the priestly ministry (*ministerium sacerdotum*) should not lack means to offer sacrifices (*ad hostias salutares*) for the people's welfare, and perform the sacred rites more frequently.'

The whole emphasis of the preface is on the subordinate role of the presbyters as assistants to the bishop in leading, teaching and sanctifying. The priest's role at the eucharist is not emphasized but is clearly symbolized. It was this symbolism that Cranmer was to change in his reformed Ordinal.

The imposition of the stole, which followed the preface, did not precisely symbolize cult but rather the yoke of the Lord and the priestly holiness which is so prominently emphasized in the prayers and symbols of the pontifical. This was true not only of Sarum but of the pontificals of Egbert and Dunstan and, later, of Bangor, Winchester, and Exeter. In the words of Sarum,

> 'Accept the yoke of the Lord: for his yoke is sweet and his burden light. May the Lord endow you with the stole of innocence.'

The imposition of the chasuble was more 'cultic' in its symbolism; but here too the emphasis in the words of the rite was that this 'priestly' vestment signified holiness. After placing the chasuble over his shoulder the bishop said to each of the newly ordained:

> 'Take this priestly vestment, the symbol of charity; God has the power to give you increase of charity and in you bring his work to perfection.'

The prayer of 'consecration' which followed these medieval additions again emphasized the desired virtue in priests and compared them to the presbyters appointed by Timothy and Titus. They are to be elders in gravity and example. They are to meditate upon God's law, believing what they read, teaching what they believe, and living what they teach. They are to be examples of justice, mercy, constancy, fortitude, poverty, charity, faith, pure conscience, and of all other virtues. This prayer also refers briefly to their ministry at the altar.

'Theirs be the task to change with blessing undefiled, for the service of thy people, the bread and wine into the body and blood of thy Son.'

After the hymn *Veni Creator* there was an optional prayer for the blessing of the priest's hands. This prayer was rich in sacrificial imagery.

'Bless and sanctify, Lord, these hands of your priests for consecrating offerings which are offered for the sins and imperfections of people; and for blessing other things which are necessary. . . .'

The blessing and anointing of the hands with oil, a ceremony which originally signified holiness and the power to bless, had in the middle ages become closely associated with the eucharist.

'Be pleased, Lord, to consecrate and sanctify these hands by this anointing and our blessing, that whatever they consecrate may be consecrated and whatever they bless may be blessed and sanctified.'

Immediately after this rite there followed the most fateful and significant of all the medieval additions to the ordination service — the *porrectio instrumentorum,* the presentation of sacred vessels signifying the priest's power at the eucharist. The presiding bishop presented a paten with wafers and a chalice with wine while saying the following words which unequivocally reflected Catholic belief in the eucharist as a propitiatory sacrifice for the quick and the dead.

'Receive the power to offer sacrifice to God, and to celebrate Mass, both for the living and the dead.'

Immediately before the postcommunion prayer there was another medieval addition, a *second* imposition of hands, accompanied by these familiar words.

'Receive the Holy Ghost. Whose sins you shall remit they are remitted. Whose you shall retain they are retained.'

After lowering their chasubles and exchanging the kiss of peace the bishop requested the prayers of the newly ordained. He also gave a final blessing which, like the presentation of the instruments, was clearly and explicitly sacrificial in its emphasis.

> 'May the blessing of God the Father, the Son and the Holy Ghost descend upon you, that you may be blessed in the sacerdotal order, and that you may offer pleasing sacrifices to God for the sins and offences of the people to almighty God to whom is honour and glory forever. Amen.'

A final brief admonition once again demonstrates late medieval belief in the importance of the priest's role at the eucharist. The admonition was doubtless necessary where there were ignorant parsons, but the absence of any reference to the other sacraments and to preaching and teaching is significant.

> 'Because the things you are to perform are so serious, beloved brethren, I admonish that you learn diligently and seriously from well instructed priests the order of the whole Mass, and the consecration, and fraction, and communion before you presume to sing Mass.'

The archdeacon then enjoined upon the new priests nine masses, three of the Trinity, three of Our Lady, and three requiem masses. The bishop announced a forty days indulgence for all who 'heard' these first masses. The Sarum pontifical concludes with the rubric that the above ceremony is to be used in all general ordinations.

This then was the ordination rite for priests in pre-reformation England. Some parts of it had displeased Wyclif and the later reformers. Many of its prayers explicitly signified sacrificial priesthood. Yet it remained a rite that reflected belief in the priest as a co-operator with other priests and, above all, with the bishop or high priest. It emphasized the need for priestly virtue and holiness and it stressed his functions of leadership, preaching and teaching. It remained a comprehensive norm of belief and prayer in substantial continuity with the Roman and Gallican rites from which it had developed. But in every authorized liturgy there is a continuous dialogue between the official liturgy and popular belief. The liturgy nourished and reflected belief; and belief influenced the liturgy. As J.M. Tillard has written, 'the first step towards understanding what a church conceives the ministry in fact to be is to make a close study of its rites of ordination'. But he also remarks, 'the sacraments belong within the living faith (of a church) and derive their ultimate meaning from that faith'. [18]

Therefore the theology and mass system of a particular period are important for understanding the conception of a church's ministry as expressed in its ordination rites. Anglican apologists are doubtless correct that the late medieval liturgy cannot be studied in isolation from the stipendiary abuses, pluralism, and popular superstition about the efficacy of a vast *quantity* of chantry masses for the deceased; nor can the liturgy be studied in isolation from large currents of the popular 'theology' of a period. [19] Several medieval additions to the English rite were incorporated into the liturgy in awkward juxtaposition with more venerable actions and prayers. While the earliest ordination rites we possess do symbolize the priest's role in the eucharistic memorial, [20] later additions by emphasizing his power of consecration and sacrifice reflect and encourage the conception of the priest as primarily an offerer of propitiatory sacrifice for the quick and the dead. [21]

Nevertheless, when taken as a whole within its historical context, the Sarum Ordinal teaches orthodox faith in the priest-hood. We have already noticed that the Sarum Ordinal reflected a more comprehensive concept of priesthood than Anglican apologists have sometimes admitted. In brief, the Ordinal embodies the centuries old faith in the priest as the representative

[18] J.M. Tillard, 'Roman Catholics and Anglicans: the Eucharist', *One in Christ*, Vol. IX, no. 2, 1973, pp. 181, 190-191.

[19] J.J. Hughes, *Stewards of the Lord*, pp. 42-98; Francis Clark, *Eucharistic Sacrifice and the Reformation*, pp. 56-73; K.L. Wand-Legh, *Perpetual Chantries in Britain*, Cambridge, 1965, pp. 312-313; H. Maynard Smith, *Henry VIII and the Reformation*, London, 1962, pp. 406-408.

[20] David Power, *Ministers of Christ and His Church*, pp. 31-41, esp. 39-41; P. Grelot, *Le Ministere de la Nouvelle Alliance*, Paris, 1967, pp. 122-142.

[21] *The Ordination Prayers of the Ancient Western Churches*, H.B. Porter, ed., pp. 78-87.

of Christ who is called by God to lead and unify his people and whose ministry is authenticated through episcopal ordination. The priest represents Christ as priest, leader and teacher; and priestly holiness is of paramount importance. He is associated with other priests and is an assistant to the episcopal order. The priest had power to bless and forgive and to confect and offer the eucharist. The power of jurisdiction and ordering was reserved to the bishop.

The Consecration of Bishops

The norm of belief reflected in the consecration ceremony has fewer explicit references to sacrifice than does the ordination rite for priests. We shall examine the consecration rite in conjunction with the ordination ceremony in order to understand the sixteenth century belief in priesthood. Although we shall emphasize those parts of the rite which explicitly pertain to sacrifice it should be remembered that the rite as a whole was comprehensive in its teaching.

The Sarum consecration rite for bishops begins with a rubric that the bishop elect must provide the necessary vestments, ring, staff, mitre and paraphernalia used in episcopal consecrations.

According to a custom extending back to the fifth century the consecration of bishops took place on the Sabbath. According to Sarum, however, the consecration was preceded by a detailed examination of the elect which did not invariably take place on the day of consecration and was, moreover, a relatively late addition to the rite, first appearing in England in the eleventh century. The entire examination is pertinent to our study because it reflects a comprehensive concept of the episcopal office. While there is an explicit and detailed examination of the elect's belief in the real presence this is but one aspect of the examination and was not emphasized. We shall recount this particular section in detail because, as Eric Mascall has correctly argued, 'I cannot agree with those who hold that without a satisfactory doctrine of the presence an adequate understanding of the sacrifice is either adequate or sufficient.' [22]

---

[22] Eric Mascall, *Corpus Christi*, London, 1965, p. 83.

After recalling the Pauline injunction to impose hands on no unworthy person the metropolitan or presiding prelate queried the elect about his intention to adhere to the sacred scriptures, to which the elect replied, 'I so wish, from my whole heart, to obey and consent to them in all things.' Then he was examined on his willingness to teach the scriptures in example as well as word and to accept, teach and obey the traditions of the orthodox fathers and the decretals of the Apostolic See. He was asked about his intention to remain loyal to the See of Canterbury, his metropolitan and his successors according to canonical authority and the decrees of the Pope. At this point the examination was interrupted so that the bishop elect could make a solemn profession of due reverence, subjection and obedience to the Archbishop of Canterbury, his metropolitan and their successors and to do all 'according to the decrees of the Roman pontiff and your laws.' [23]

After this solemn profession the examination resumed. The bishop elect was asked if he intended to live an exemplary life of chastity and sobriety, if he would engage in divine pursuits and abstain from the pursuit of wealth, if he would live and teach a life of humility and patience and if he would assist the poor and needy. This part of the examination — to which the bishop elect repeatedly answered 'volo' — was terminated by a brief invocation of the presiding bishop to which the congregation replied 'Amen'.

The examination then resumed with the central dogmas of the Catholic faith. The bishop elect was asked to profess his faith in the Trinity and the Creation, in the divinity of Christ and in his eternal origin from the Father and his earthly birth from the Virgin Mary, in the one divine Person and two complete natures, in the passion, death, resurrection, ascension, session and final judgment, in the full divinity and twofold

---

[23] This part of the profession became, of course, a bone of contention when royal supremacy became an issue. Maskell remarks that in an ancient pontifical which he examined, the traditional phrase was erased and there was substituted in the margin, 'according to the laws and statutes of this kingdom', in Maskell, *Monumenta Ritualia*, p. 263, note 19. Cf. also Jasper Ridley, *Thomas Cranmer*, pp. 55-58.

procession of the Holy Spirit, and in the one Godhead of the Trinity. The elect was asked if he believed that the holy, Catholic and apostolic church was the one true church in which is given the one baptism and true remission of sins. To all these dogmas the bishop elect responded 'Credo'.

Within the examination about his faith in the church there was included a question about his belief in the substantial change and real presence in the eucharist, the ancient belief of the Catholic church in the new, true and real presence of Christ in the Lord's Supper. Because of its importance for our study we record this part of the examination in full. [24]

> 'Question: Do you believe that the bread which is placed on the Lord's table, is only bread before consecration: but in that consecration, by the ineffable power of the Divinity, the nature and substance of that bread is changed into the nature and substance of the flesh of Christ, of no other flesh but that which was conceived of the Holy Spirit and born from the Virgin Mary?
>
> Response: I believe.
>
> Question: Similarly, the wine which mixed with water is put forward in the chalice to be sanctified, truly and essentially to be converted into the blood, which through the sword of a soldier flowed from the wound of the side of the Lord.
>
> Response: I believe.'

The examination continued with the bishop elect's promise to anathematize every heresy against the Catholic church, and with his profession of faith in the resurrection of the flesh and eternal life and in the divine authorship of the bible. The presiding bishop concluded this preliminary part of the consecration ceremony with a final brief invocation to which all present

---

[24] These two interrogations are included in the Winchester pontifical but are omitted in the Exeter and Bangor uses. Cf. Maskell, *Monumenta Ritualia*, p. 265, note 21.

responded 'Amen'. 'May this faith be increased in you by God, most beloved brother, unto true and eternal beatitude.'

With the successful completion of this examination and with the consent of the laity, clerics and bishops of the province and of the metropolitan the bishop elect was 'ordained in the name of the Lord'.

The consecration ceremony began with the mass of the day and included a special petition that what followed would be efficacious through the power of God. During the preparatory prayers the bishop-elect was vested with sandals, alb, stole, maniple, tunic, dalmatic and chasuble but not with mitre, staff nor ring. After the gradual the presiding bishop ascended the altar and sat facing the choir. Two bishops led the bishop elect to the archbishop's chair. It was at this part of the ceremony that there was an explicit reference to the bishop as an offerer of sacrifice when the archbishop said,

'It is the office of the bishop to judge, to interpret, to consecrate, to confirm, to order, to offer, and to baptize.'

There followed a bidding prayer on behalf of the ordained and the customary litany with three special invocations for his blessing, sanctification and consecration. The bible was placed over the head and shoulders of the elect while the archbishop blessed him and with the other bishops imposed hands upon his head. The archbishop intoned the *Veni Creator* which was followed by the ancient Roman prayer for sacerdotal grace.

'Be gracious, oh Lord, to our supplications and with the horn of priestly grace inclined over these thy servants, pour out upon them the power of thy benediction.'

The preface was almost identical with the traditional prayer which had been in use for a thousand years. However, in the middle ages the ancient analogy comparing the bishop to Aaron the high priest had come to reflect and influence a more sacrificial emphasis than when it was originally used in the fifth century. This part of the ceremony must be studied with the later medieval theology of the priest and bishop as offerers of sacrifice in mind. Similarly the medieval understanding of priestly vestments as connected with the eucharist and the late medieval mass system should be considered. [25] For here we have an example of the dialogue between popular belief and practice and the teaching of the liturgy. Aaron was still a type of the later priesthood and his vestments still signified holiness. But within its sixteenth century context — as we shall see it illustrated in the theology of Stephen Gardiner — the Aaronic symbolism was viewed in a more sacrificial way than the ancient words portraying it would indicate. Nevertheless, the prayer itself and the entire consecration ceremony is comprehensive and reflects a comprehensive concept of the high priesthood. What is most emphasized is the bishop's leadership and holiness. The most cognate parts of the preface are as follows.

> 'God who holding private familiar converse with thy servant Moses hast also decreed, among the other patterns of heavenly worship, concerning the disposition of priestly vesture; and didst command that Moses thy servant should wear a mystical robe during the sacred rites, so that the posterity to come would have an understanding of the meaning of the former things, lest the knowledge of thy teaching be lost in any age and as the very outward sign of these symbols obtained reverence among thy former folk, also among us there might be a knowledge of them more certain than types and symbols. For the adornment of our mind is as the vesture of that earlier priesthood; and the dignity of robes no longer commends to us the pontifical glory, but rather the splendour of spirits. . . . And therefore to these thy servants to whom thou hast chosen for the ministry of high priesthood, we beseech thee oh Lord that thou should grant this grace and that whatsoever it was that those veils signified in radiance of gold, in sparkling of jewels, in variety of divine workmanship, this may show forth in the conversation and deeds of these men . . .'

The emphasis of the prayer, therefore, is on leadership, a leadership and high priesthood that is exercised primarily through the 'authority' of sanctity, fidelity, purity, faith, love, sincerity and peace. Nor was there any explicit allusion to sacrifice in the anointing of the new bishop's head with oil.

---

[25] Power, *Ministers of Christ and His Church*, pp. 87-106.

> 'May your head be anointed and consecrated with heavenly
> blessing, in the pontifical order, through the unction of
> holy oil and charism and our blessing.'

The prayer subsequent to this first anointing was almost identical
with the ancient Roman rite. Here too the emphasis was on the
bishop's holiness and leadership. There was also a significant
insertion from the ancient Gallican rite.

> 'Give them, oh Lord, the keys of the kingdom of heaven.
> Let them use what thou hast given for edification not for
> destruction, neither let them glory in power. Whatsoever
> they bind on earth, let it be bound also in heaven; and
> whatsoever they loose on earth, let it also be loosed in
> heaven. Whose sins they may retain, let them be retained,
> and whose sins they may forgive, do thou forgive.'

There followed another consecration prayer which had been
added to the English rite in the middle ages and was still in use
in the sixteenth century. [26] This prayer, recalling God's promises
to Abraham, refers to the bishop's high priesthood, beseeching
God,

> 'that this thy servant may be worthy in the services and
> all the functions faithfully performed, that so he may be
> able to celebrate the mysteries of the sacraments ordained
> of old. By thee may he be consecrated unto the high
> priesthood to which he is lifted up.'

The emphasis is on the bishop's holiness and example. He is to
be a model of justice and fidelity, a bestower of heavenly gifts,
kind, charitable, hospitable, courageous, patient and truthful.
He is to oppose heresy and schism and all other vices, to be a
just judge and learned teacher. He is admitted to the priesthood
which is a task and not a privilege and which, faithfully exercised,
will eventuate in his admission to the heavenly kingdom.

> 'May he reckon priesthood itself to be a task and not a
> privilege. May increase of honour come to him, to the
> encouragement of his merits also, that through these, as
> with us now he is admitted to the priesthood, so with thee
> hereafter he may be admitted to the kingdom.'

---

[26] Maskell, *Monumenta Ritualia*, p. 285, note 38.

C

The bishop therefore was a successor of Aaron, the high priest of the new people of God. This was symbolized even more explicitly with the repetition of the antiphon about the ointment which flowed onto the head, beard and vestments of Aaron. The prayer accompanying the anointing of the bishop's hands recalled again the analogy with Aaron. In addition it compared the bishop to the apostles who were anointed by the Spirit. The bishop therefore was both high priest and successor of the apostles. His hands were anointed for sanctification but also for the power of blessing and consecrating.

> 'Whatever you bless may it be blessed and whatever you sanctify may it be sanctified; and may the imposition of your consecrated hand or finger be profitable to all for salvation.'

The various blessings of the new bishop's symbols of office all pray for his sanctification. The blessing of the staff is accompanied by a prayer for his justice, clemency and fairness in ruling. The episcopal ring signifies holiness and the marriage of the bishop to the church. The mitre symbolizes good works, interior virtue and is given with a petition for the bishop's salvation.

The Sarum consecration ceremony concludes with the bestowal of the gospels accompanied with the following words.

> 'Accept the gospel and go and preach to the people committed to you. For God is powerful to increase in you his grace who lives and reigns forever and ever.'

The ceremony concluded, the archbishop continued with the mass for the day while two bishops accompanied the newly consecrated high priest to another altar where he celebrated the mass of Our Lady. [27]

Conclusion

While the belief in priesthood reflected in the Sarum pontifical is comprehensive and in substantial continuity with Catholic belief reaching back to apostolic times, some medieval additions

---

[27] *Ibid.*, p. 293, note 45.

such as anointing, vesting, and the giving of instruments, tended to emphasize the minister's role at the altar.

The analogies in Sarum with Aaron and levitical priesthood, with the elders who assisted Moses, with the apostles and their disciples had been within the ordination rites since patristic times. In the middle ages attention became focused on the analogy with Jewish priesthood and therefore on sacrifice, but in the liturgy the other venerable analogies which signified the hierarchy's functions of teaching and leading were maintained.

The liturgy, including the ordination rites, is a norm and mirror of belief. But it is a conservative norm and mirror. Decades and even centuries may pass before developments in doctrine and practice find their way into the public prayer of the church. Therefore it seems that in the late middle ages a more cultic emphasis on priesthood was read into the liturgy than was explicitly symbolized in its prayers and actions.

Even with this qualification, however, the central belief of the English people in the meaning of priesthood may be found in the Sarum pontifical. And that belief was that the priest represented Christ as pastor and teacher as well as president at the Lord's Supper. What the Sarum rite *did* emphasize in almost every page was the desired holiness and example of bishops, priests and deacons. Their leadership, preaching and teaching were exercised primarily through the holiness of their lives. The 'authority' of the hierarchy emphasized in Sarum was authority in that ancient sense which transcends mere power. The minister's function at the eucharist symbolized his authoritative function in the community.

What Cranmer and the reformers objected to was the liturgy's emphasis, especially in the medieval additions to the pontifical, on sacrifice which in its turn reflected and influenced popular belief. It was this emphasis which Cranmer and his colleagues wanted to change. However in altering the rites — mainly through omission — Cranmer and the reformers reacted not only against late medieval abuses but against the centuries old belief of the church that the priesthood did in fact reach its climax and fulfilment when the minister represented Christ and his people at the eucharistic memorial.

This traditional and orthodox belief of the English people is illustrated not only in the pontifical but also in the writings of Stephen Gardiner who, during the two most crucial decades of the Tudor reformation and restoration, was the acknowledged leader of the conservative party in the church of England. [28] It is to Gardiner's teaching that we now turn.

[28] A.G. Dickens, *The English Reformation*, London, 1966, pp. 174-178.

CHAPTER II

Stephen Gardiner

'Unto some God hath committed the office of teaching and the ministry of the sacraments.'   Stephanus Winton

Stephen Gardiner, who grew up in the environs of the mighty abbey of Bury St Edmunds, never deviated from the traditional belief in priesthood and eucharist in common possession in England before the reformation.

As Master of Trinity Hall and Chancellor of Cambridge, secretary to Henry VIII, lawyer, canonist, diplomat and theologian, dogged defender of the old faith (with the temporary exception of the papal supremacy), foe of innovation, prisoner under Edward VI, and Lord Chancellor under Mary Tudor, the bishop of Winchester throughout the vicissitudes of his turbulent times was the acknowledged spokesman of the conservative party in England.

With the endemic caution of the trained jurist Gardiner was always suspicious of novelty — not excluding the royal supremacy — and he consistently upheld Catholic teaching on episcopacy, the Mass and priesthood. Because of his astute advocacy of traditional doctrine his enemies labelled him 'popish lawyer' while his supporters compared him to Cicero in his eloquent and erudite treatises defending the faith. [1] To his

---

[1] James A. Muller, *Stephen Gardiner and the Tudor Reaction*, London, 1926, p. 7.

23

partisans Gardiner's theological writings were the able exposition and defence of their Catholicism, to his opponents he was a wily and skilful adversary. [2]

Born in 1497 Gardiner enjoyed, as an adolescent, a brief sojourn in Paris, a 'moveable feast' that prepared him for future diplomatic ventures on the continent. Although his main subject at Cambridge was the law he also familiarized himself with the humanities, classical languages and theology. [3]

Gardiner entered public life as part of Henry VIII's entourage. At the age of thirty-three he was already principal secretary to the King. In May, 1530, he examined, along with such other conservatives as More, Warham and Tunstall, several suspect books including Tyndale's translation of scripture — and found them wanting. [4] Partly because of his learning and conservatism and partly because of his skill as a courtier Gardiner was in 1531, at the age of thirty-four, elected Bishop of Winchester by the King and approved in that prestigious office by the Pope.

In the same year 'Stephen Winton' concurred in the condemnation of John Frith for the latter's denial of transubstantiation, the real presence and purgatory. In 1535, with some misgivings, Gardiner accepted the Act of Supremacy and wrote a defence of the King's authority in matters ecclesiastical. [5] But he failed to induce John Fisher to travel the same road. 'Fisher was falsely informed that More had taken the oath, but he remained firm — as he did when various bishops, including Tunstall and Gardiner, tried to persuade him.' [6] In a distasteful tract concerning Fisher's subsequent execution Gardiner wrote,

> 'The churche is helpyd and nott woundyd, by the deth of
> a trayter . . . in the last ende of his lif, when he agaynst

[2] *Ibid.*, p. 297.

[3] *Ibid.*, p. 7.

[4] *Ibid.*, p. 41.

[5] Stephen Gardiner, 'The Oration of True Obedience', *Obedience in Church and State, Three Political Tracts by Stephen Gardiner,* Pierre Jannelle, ed., N.Y., 1968, pp. 67-173.

[6] Edward Surtz, *The Works and Days of John Fisher* (1469-1535), Cambridge, 1967, p. 27.

all lawes as well of god, as of men, resistyd his prince,
and the ordinance of god, and beyng also a traitor, was
imprisoned therfore, he was then incontinently esteemed
of thatt holy see worthye to bee a cardinall.' [7]

This was not one of Gardiner's finest hours. As the reformation
quickened, especially in its 'Jacobin stage', [8] Gardiner began to
harbour second thoughts about the wisdom and rectitude of
royal supremacy. At the Ratisbon diet of 1541 Gardiner, with
the sole exception of the supremacy, was according to the
Venetian ambassador consistently on the Catholic side. [9] A.J.
Slavin observes that from as early as 1536 Bishop Longland
of Lincoln 'stood with Gardiner and the conservatives', [10] clearly
implying Gardiner's leadership of the Catholic faction.

In May, 1543, the so-called 'King's Book' appeared, a
relatively conservative document in which Gardiner's positions
on priesthood and eucharist were endorsed. In the words of
James Muller, Gardiner's biographer, the book was 'the most
successful attempt in the reformation age — perhaps in any age
— to set forth a doctrinal exposition of anti-papal Catholicism'.[11]
Indeed as Henry's health faded in the last three years of his
reign the defence of 'anti-papal Catholicism', including the
defence of clerical celibacy against Martin Bucer, occupied a
substantial part of Gardiner's time. [12]

When death released Henry's iron grasp the bishop of
Winchester, soon out of favour with the protectorate, fell back
on the stratagem of counselling no religious innovation during

[7] Stephen Gardiner, 'Tract on Fisher's Execution', in *Obedience in
Church and State,* pp. 30-31.
[8] As it is called by the Anglican scholar T.M. Parker, *The English
Reformation to 1558,* Oxford, 1950.
[9] H. Maynard Smith, *Henry VIII and the English Reformation,*
London, 1962, pp. 184-185.
[10] *Thomas Cromwell on Church and Commonwealth,* Arthur J. Slavin,
ed., N.Y., 1969, p. 137, note.
[11] J.A. Muller, *Stephen Gardiner,* p. 107.
[12] 'To Somerset, 28 February, 1547', in *The Letters of Stephen
Gardiner,* J.A. Muller, ed., Cambridge, 1933, pp. 265-266.
[13] Bucer was a favourite target of Gardiner's. Cf. 'Gardiner's Answer
to Bucer', in *Obedience in Church and State,* pp. 173-212.

the boy king's minority. [13] His tenacity resulted in four month's imprisonment in the fleet. When released he continued to discountenance innovation although he consented to the insertion of Cranmer's vernacular 'Order of the Communion' into the missals of his diocese. [14] But he was delated for preaching the true and real presence in the eucharist and was imprisoned in the Tower.

On St Peter's Day, 1548, in a command performance Gardiner preached before the King and council at Whitehall. In refined and guarded language he defended traditional Catholic teaching on the Mass. According to a transcription of his words preserved by John Foxe the prisoner drew an analogy between Christ and the bishops. Christ acted as high priest or bishop in offering his all-sufficient sacrifice for the sins of the world; it is the office of bishops to offer memorials of that sacrifice. [15] Gardiner's utterances on the eucharist enraged Protector Somerset who remanded him to the tower. When commanded to endorse the 1549 Communion Service Gardiner temporized and then refused. Later, with a solicitor's skill, he argued that the rite contained orthodox teaching. [16] Gardiner never denied the true, real and 'very' presence of Christ in the eucharist, a crime for which he was deprived of his bishopric. [17] While in the Tower he remained non-commital on the 1550 Ordinal except to comment that he disapproved of the omission of anointing. Four years later, however, in a sermon before the Queen and Reginald Pole, Gardiner argued that those 'ordered' by Cranmer's Ordinals were not true priests but were 'lay, profane and married.' [18]

During his five years in the tower Gardiner wrote several theological treatises including works against Oecolampadius, Bucer, Hooper and Cranmer. In 1550 Cranmer's *Defence of the True and Catholic Doctrine and Use of the Sacrament of the*

[14] J.A. Muller, *Stephen Gardiner,* pp. 158-160.
[15] John Foxe, *Acts and Monuments,* Josiah Pratt, ed., London, Vol. VI, pp. 89-90.
[16] J.A. Muller, *Stephen Gardiner,* p. 188.
[17] *Ibid.,* pp. 201-202.
[18] *Epistolarum Reginaldi Poli,* Pars V, p. 296.

Lord's Supper appeared as an answer to Gardiner's defence of
the traditional doctrine in his St Peter's Day sermon and other
writings. [19] Gardiner promptly replied with *An Explicitation and
Assertion of the True Catholic Faith, Touching the Most Blessed
Sacrament of the Altar, With Confutation of a Book Written
Against the Same.* Cranmer countered with his major and final
eucharistic work including his *Defence* and Gardiner's *Explicita-
tion and Assertion.* This book is for our purposes Cranmer's
most important because it is his last and because it is contemporary with his revision of his Ordinal. It was entitled *An
Answer Unto a Crafty and Sophistical Cavillation Devised by
Stephen Gardiner Against the True and Godly Doctrine of the
Most Holy Sacrament of the Body and Blood of Our Saviour
Jesus Christ.* Gardiner wrote a response in Latin, *Confutatio
Cavillationum,* first printed in 1552 in Paris under the pen name
of Marcus Constantius and in 1554 in Louvain under Gardiner's
own name. Cranmer's rejoinder was neither completed nor
published because of his imprisonment and death in the reign
of Mary Tudor. [20]

In 1553 soon after Edward VI's death Gardiner, still the
recognized leader of the conservatives, was liberated by the new
Queen and restored to his bishopric and Cambridge offices. He
offered a Latin Mass for the late King and later presided at
Mary's coronation. In March, 1554, Gardiner, now Lord
Chancellor, had a prominent part in the authorship of some
articles on religion. Included was the significant clause that
persons ordered during Edward's reign 'considering they were
not ordered in very deed' were to have what was wanting in
their orders supplied by a bishop before he permitted them to
minister. [21] The meaning of this vague article is not completely
clear. We cannot say categorically whether or not Gardiner
believed the new ordering 'null, void and invalid' or whether he
believed it 'irregular and illicit'. However, Gardiner's endorse-

---

[19] *Archbishop Cranmer on the True and Catholic Doctrine and Use
of the Sacrament of the Lord's Supper,* Charles H.H. Wright, ed.,
London, 1907.
[20] John Strype, *Memorials of Archbishop Cranmer,* 3 Vols., Oxford,
1848, Vol. II, pp. 326-328.
[21] J.A. Muller, *Stephen Gardiner,* p. 250 and note.

ment of the article demonstrates that, at a minimum, the leading spokesman for the conservative party in England had reservations about 'Anglican Orders'.

Gardiner made no objections to Reginald Pole's return to England and his installation as primate. He confessed his error in professing and defending the royal supremacy. He never had wavered and never would in his defence of traditional Catholic teaching on purgatory, the Mass and the priesthood. He was only consistent when in his last will and testament he left £400 'for the erection of a chantry that I might be prayed for'. [22] Gardiner admitted that the chantry system had been abused and that *errant* chantries were rightfully dissolved; but he always taught that priests offered masses for the dead and that chantries were not in themselves evil.

Gardiner's Teaching Comprehensive

In our study of the Sarum pontifical we observed that during the late middle ages the Catholic concept of priesthood was, despite late medieval insertions into the Ordinal, comprehensive. Since the reformation studies of the ministry have focused on sacrifice and the real presence because these were — and in many cases still are — the points at issue between Roman Catholics and other Western churches. [23] In the calmer atmosphere of ecumenical convergence it is important to observe how comprehensive Catholic doctrine on the priesthood has been. [24]

Even when defending the novelty of royal supremacy Gardiner defended traditional teaching that bishops and priests were *leaders* with God-given authority to rule God's people.

---

[22] *Ibid.,* p. 290. Gardiner recognized that chantries could be abused if recourse to them were substituted for a pious life. Because they *had* been abused he supported Henry VIII's dissolution of them. Yet he always defended the orthodoxy of the chantry system, of masses and prayers for the dead when this was correctly interpreted. Cf. Foxe, *Acts and Monuments,* Vol. VI, pp. 204, 233.

[23] Edward P. Echlin, *The Anglican Eucharist in Ecumenical Perspective,* pp. vii-viii.

[24] Edward P. Echlin, *The Deacon in the Church, Past and Future,* Staten Island, 1971, pp. 97-108.

'The government of the church is committed to the
apostles and to those that succeed in their roles may not
to be thought to abrogate or diminish that that God hath
committed unto princes in any condition. The parson,
vicar or the parish priest's cure of his parishoners is never
the less because the bishop ought also to oversee; neither
may the bishop's jurisdiction be deemed of no effect
because he must take the archbishop for his superior. For
the curate, the bishop and the archbishop do govern the
church every one in their degree and order.' [25]

In a tract against Bucer Gardiner acknowledged that Peter was
'prince' of the apostles and that bishops, as successors of the
apostles, were leaders in the church. [26] It is clear from the
register of Gardiner's diocese that in his teaching bishops enjoyed
certain powers that priests do not share.

'To the Catholic bishop for celebrating and conferring the
aforesaid orders, all and each, in our diocese at the appropriate time according to the statutes, and for anointing and
confirming the baptized, and for blessing and sanctifying
holy oil and chrism and for consecrating and reconciling
churches, chapels and cemeteries in our diocese, for
blessing and sanctifying vestments, chalices and bells and
other and all things which pertain to the order and character of the office of bishop. . . ' [27]

Priests did more than celebrate Mass. They baptized and
reconciled, presided at the other sacraments, gave many blessings
and, very important, prayed for their people.

'All this honour is given to man, as spiritually to regenerate,
when the minister sayeth "I baptize thee", and to remit
sin to such as fall after, to be also a minister in consecration
of Christ's most precious body, with the ministration of
other sacraments, benedictions and prayer.' [28]

---

[25] 'The Oration of True Obedience', in *Obedience in Church and
State,* p. 103; cf. 'To Paget' 1 March, 1547, in *Letters,* p. 269.

[26] 'Answer to Martin Bucer', *Ibid.,* p. 179.

[27] *Registra Stephani Gardiner et Joannis Poynet,* Herbert Chitty, ed.,
Oxford, 1930, p. 12.

[28] 'An Explicitation and Assertion of the True Catholic Faith, Touching the Most Blessed Sacrament of the Altar, With Confutation of

Nor did Gardiner neglect the primary duty of the minister to preach and teach the gospel. He complained bitterly when Somerset restricted the episcopal office of preaching throughout a diocese. 'At this time bishops be restrained by a special policy to preach only in their Cathedral churches (the like whereof hath not been known in my time).' [29]

The hierarchy were ministers of *the word* as well as of the sacraments.

> 'Forasmuch as government has need of many things especially teaching and preeminence according to the sundry distribution of gifts, unto some God hath committed the office of teaching and the ministry of the sacraments. . .' [30]

However Gardiner seemed dissatisfied with the *quality* of preaching. One of his arguments against the introduction of official homilies was that few Englishmen listened even to the spontaneous homilies of their priests. He thought Englishmen poor listeners who would listen even less if homilies were *read*. 'So it is in preaching, and especially where the man is not esteemed, as priests be not, and should be less if they fell a talking: for so they would call it, to rehearse an homily made by another.' [31]

Although Gardiner thought the early church somewhat harsh in its use of excommunications he professed that bishops and priests, as ministers of the word, did possess the power to excommunicate. He interpreted the popular symbol of the first sword as follows: 'By the one sword, alluding to the saying of Paul, which the ministers of the word exercise in preaching and excommunicating.' [32]

---

a Book Written Against the Same', in *Writings and Disputations of Thomas Cranmer Relative to the Sacrament of the Lord's Supper,* John Cox, ed., (Parker Society), Cambridge, 1844, p. 83; cf. p. 227. Gardiner's tract is reprinted by Cranmer in his answer to the same.

[29] 'To Somerset', 6 June, 1547, in *Letters,* p. 289.

[30] 'The Oration of True Obedience', in *Obedience in Church and State,* p. 103.

[31] 'To Cranmer', c. 12 June, 1547, in *Letters,* p. 315; cf. 'To Cromwell', 10 June, 1535, *Ibid.,* p. 66, and 'To Ridley', 28 February, 1547, *Ibid.,* p. 258.

[32] *Ibid.,* p. 107.

As was clearly emphasized in the Sarum Ordinal bishops and priests were to be virtuous. Henry VIII commissioned Gardiner as bishop of Winchester to ordain only virtuous men. Because priests were ministers of the word it was equally important that they be learned.

> 'Never promote anyone at any time to holy orders, nor admit them to the care of souls, unless they are approved by the most certain testimonials for so great and venerable a function by the integrity of their lives and their knowledge of letters.' [33]

Years later when Henry was dead and Gardiner out of favour and in the tower he wrote in words similar to the Sarum Ordinal about the virtues requisite in a priest and cited Jerome on the holiness and chastity necessary in a bishop.

> 'As meekness, patience, sobriety, moderation, abstinence of gain, hospitality also, and liberality should be chiefly in a bishop, and among all laymen and excellency in them; so there should be in him a special chastity, and, as I should say, chastity that is priestly...' [34]

As devout and learned preachers bishops were guardians of the apostolic tradition. Gardiner 'practised what he preached' even though his doctrinal fidelity led him to the fleet and, eventually, the tower. As early as 1547 he wrote to the Privy Council objecting to their doctrinal innovations and asserting his episcopal function to guard the deposit, 'to lay before you even the platform of my inward determination, which is to preserve the flock committed unto me as a true bishop'. [35] Gardiner considered himself exercising this episcopal duty when he disputed with Martin Bucer. 'Of my charge as a bishop I shall render my account to God — would that it were such as I wish. Meanwhile as long as I spend time, wherever it may be, in confuting and rebutting you, meseems I am not away from my flock.' [36]

---

[33] *Registra,* p. 49.
[34] 'Explicitation and Assertion', in *Writings and Disputations of Thomas Cranmer,* p. 193; cf. p. 194.
[35] 'To the Privy Council', 30 August, 1547, *Letters,* p. 372.
[36] 'Answer to Martin Bucer', in *Obedience in Church and State,* p. 211.

We have noticed that, with the exception of the royal
supremacy, Gardiner was the principal spokesman of the Catholic
party. He was conservative in more than dogma. He stoutly
defended clerical celibacy especially in his dispute with Bucer.

> 'God compels no-one to celibacy, but as for those which
> have made themselves eunuchs for the kingdom of heaven's
> sake, he does not allow them to change their resolve to
> the scandal of others, and to despise their vows. The
> freedom of marriage is open to all, but not to such
> eunuchs.' [37]

The power of Christ the invisible priest was effective through
his minister, the visible priest on earth.

> '[Christ] sitting in heaven doth, as our invisible priest,
> work in the ministry of the visible priesthood of his church,
> and maketh present by his omnipotency his glorified body
> and blood, in this high mystery, by the conversion of the
> visible creatures of bread and wine.' [38]

These words provide an apt transition to Gardiner's defence of
the traditional teaching on the priesthood in its connection with
the eucharist. Every theologian and bishop is of necessity engaged
in the primary problematics of his own brief period in history. [39]
In Gardiner's time controversy swirled around the eucharist. It
should be clear, however, from the preceeding pages that for
Gardiner, for Sarum, and for the Catholic tradition which the
bishop-theologian and the liturgy represented the priesthood
was not related exclusively to eucharistic sacrifice.

---

[37] *Ibid.*

[38] 'Explicitation and Assertion', in *Writings and Disputations of Thomas
Cranmer,* p. 193; cf. p. 79. It is interesting to note that Gardiner's
teaching that Christ the invisible priest worked in the sacraments
through the visible minister was repeated recently in words similar
to Gardiner's by the American Catholic bishops. More significant
still is the fact that the bishops were issuing a catechetical directory
for those teaching the true Christian faith. '[The sacraments] are
always to be thought of as action of Christ himself, from whom they
get their power. Thus it is Christ who baptizes, Christ who offers
himself in the sacrifice of the mass through the ministry of the
priests, and Christ who forgives sins in the sacrament of penance',
in National Conference of Catholic Bishops, 'Basic Teachings for
Catholic Religious Education', *The Catholic Mind,* May, 1973,
pp. 50-51.

[39] C.K. Barrett, *The Signs of An Apostle,* London, 1970, pp. 19-20.

Priesthood and the Real Presence

One of Cranmer's principal arguments against Roman Catholic teaching on the real presence was that Christ was locally in heaven; he could not be in several places at one time. Gardiner too professed the glorified presence of Christ in heaven. But he denied that Christ's heavenly presence conflicted with his presence in the eucharist.

> 'Of the very presence in deed, and therefore of the real presence of Christ's body in the Sacrament, no creature can tell how it may be, that Christ ascended into heaven with his human body, and therewith continually reigneth there, should make present in the sacrament the same body in deed, which Christ in deed worketh, being nevertheless at the same hour present then in heaven.' [40]

Repeatedly Gardiner argued that Christ the heavenly priest made himself present in the sacrament through the ministry of his visible priests. The 'how' of this new, real and very presence was a mystery which, Cranmer notwithstanding, was part of the centuries old faith.

> 'The word "corporally" may have an ambiguity and doubleness in respect and relation; one is to the truth of the body present and so it may be said, Christ is corporally present in sacrament: if the word corporally be referred to the manner of the presence, then we should say, Christ's body were present after a corporal manner, which we may not, but in a spiritual manner; and therefore not locally nor by manner of quantity, but in such manner as God only knoweth, and yet giveth us to understand by faith the truth of the very presence, exceeding our capacity to comprehend the manner "how".' [41]

In his later reply to Cranmer's *Answer* Gardiner expressed again the traditional belief of the English people in the very, true and real presence of Christ both in heaven *and* in the eucharist. 'To be in heaven and to be in the sacrament . . . nothing prohi-

---

[40] 'Explicitation and Assertion', in *Writings and Disputations by Thomas Cranmer,* pp. 340-341.

[41] *Ibid.,* p. 88; cf. also pp. 59, 73, 152, 155, 167, 189, 231.

bits to profess both. Nor by the profession of one is it necessary to deny the other.' [42]

The Swiss reformers, in Gardiner's reckoning, erred in calling the elements *mere* signs. Through a mysterious and real change wrought by Christ through the visible priest on earth the bread and wine became the very body and blood of Christ. This was the teaching of scripture and the great ecclesiastical writers. A merely symbolic presence was not the traditional teaching of the church.

> 'Christ sayith not that the bread doth only signify his body absent, nor Saint Paul saith not so in any place, nor any other canonical scripture declareth Christ's words so. As for the sense and understanding of Christ's words, there hath not been in any age any one approved and known learned man, that hath so declared and expoundeth Christ's words in the supper, that the bread did only signify Christ's body and the wine his blood, as things absent.' [43]

Gardiner, as well as Cranmer, had a better than average knowledge of scripture. The bishop of Winchester had examined Tyndale's version and found it wanting; he had himself translated parts of the gospels; and he had a lifelong interest in the Greek language. In his opinion John and Paul taught the 'very' presence of Christ and not a presence in figure only.

> 'The sixth of John speaketh not of any promise made to the eating of a token of Christ's flesh, but to the eating of Christ's very flesh, whereof the bread (as this author would have it) is but a figure in Christ's words when he said, "This is my body". And if it be but a figure in Christ's words, it is but a figure in St Paul's words, when he said, "The bread which we break is it not the communication of Christ's body?" that is to say, a figure of the communication of Christ's body (if this author's doctrine be true), and not the communication in deed.' [44]

---

[42] Stephen Gardiner, *Confutatio Cavillationum*, Louvain, 1554, p. 9; cf. also p. 2. This work was originally published in 1551 under a pen name. Cranmer's rejoinder was aborted by his imprisonment and death under Queen Mary.

[43] 'Explicitation and Assertion', in *Writings and Disputations of Thomas Cranmer*, p. 12.

[44] *Ibid.*, p. 16.

Both the reformers and the conservatives found their respective doctrines in the fathers. [45] For Gardiner, the words of the priest effected a change in the elements which, thereafter, were to be adored. The new, real and perduring presence of Christ in the eucharist was more than his presence in power in baptism.

> 'No author known and approved, that is to say Ignatius, Polycarp, Justin, Ireneus, Tertullian, Cyprian, Hilary, Chrysostom, Gregory of Nazianzene, Basil, Emissen, Ambrose, Cyril, Jerome, Augustine, Damascene, Theophylact, none of these hath this doctrine in plain terms that the bread only signifieth Christ's body absent; nor this sentence that the bread and wine be never the holier after the consecration, nor that Christ's body is none otherwise present in the sacrament but in a signification; nor this sentence, that the sacrament is not to be worshipped, because there is nothing present but in a sign.' [46]

In 1543 William Turner wrote a tract against Gardiner's traditional position. The latter replied but his answer is no longer extant. However, there are several copies available of Turner's rejoinder in which he recorded several key passages from Gardiner's tract. Turner argued that the whole Christ was not present in the bread. Gardiner replied that Christ was fully present in the bread and in the wine. Therefore he defended — as Trent would soon defend — reception by the laity of only one species.

> 'If you take it (as it seems you do not) that in one kind, of bread only, is whole Christ's body and blood, then hath the lay man nothing taken from them, but reverently abstain from other kind, the fruit whereof they receive in form of bread.' [47]

In Catholic teaching as Gardiner expressed it Christ's bodily and corporal presence was not confined to heaven. He was

---

[45] For an interesting discussion of Augustine's doctrine on symbolism and the real presence cf. J. Crehan, 'The Reformers' Eucharist', in *The Clergy Review*, July, 1959, pp. 418-424.

[46] 'Explicitation and Assertion', in *Writings and Disputations of Thomas Cranmer*, p. 13.

[47] 'Gardiner's Lost Tract Against William Turner', c. 1543, in *Letters*, p. 487.

D

'corporally' present in the eucharist. Reception of the eucharist
was a corporal eating of Christ. 'This doctrine of Christ (as I
have declared it) openeth the corporal manducation of his most
holy flesh, and drinking of his most precious blood, which he
gave in the supper under the form of bread and wine.' [48]

In Catholic teaching the corporal or carnal presence is a true
and real presence but not in a 'gross' or cannibalistic sense.
Christ's presence is 'corporal', 'natural' and 'carnal' but in a
spiritual, glorified, incorruptible sense. How this could be was
(and is) a great mystery. Gardiner wisely acknowledged that
there was a great mystery here which neither he nor any person
could fully explain.

> 'In the sacrament of the body and blood of Christ, because
> Christ is in his very true flesh present, he may be said so
> carnally present, and naturally after Hilary, and corporally
> after Cyril; understand the words of the truth of that is
> present, Christ's very body and flesh, and not of the
> manner of the presence, which is only spiritual, supernatural
> and above man's capacity: and therefore a high mystery,
> a great miracle, a wonderful work, which it is wholesome
> to believe simply with a sincere faith, and dangerous to
> search and examine with a curious imagination.' [49]

When defending transubstantiation Gardiner observed that in
Catholic teaching 'corporal' and 'natural' meant not a 'gross'
presence but a true spiritual presence.

> 'How Christ's body is in circumstances present, no man
> can define, but that it is truly present, and therefore really
> present, and not to the manner of presence which is
> spiritual, exceeding our capacity, and therefore therein
> without drawing away accidents or adding, we believe
> simply the truth...' [50]

For Gardiner, therefore, as for Thomas Aquinas, transubstantiation neither eliminated the mystery nor implied a conversion to
a 'gross' presence. On the contrary transubstantiation expressed

---

[48] 'Explicitation and Assertion', in *Writings and Disputations of Thomas
Cranmer*, p. 26.
[49] *Ibid.*, p. 189; cf. p. 239.
[50] *Ibid.*, p. 329.

a mysterious conversion whereby the material inner substance of the elements become in mystery the glorified Christ.

'For the substance of the bread and wine is an inner nature, and so is substance of one defined. And to speak of the thing changed then, as in man the change is in the soul, which is the substance of man; so for the thing changed in the visible creatures, should be also changed and is changed ... then it followeth that if the change of man's soul in baptism be true and not in a figure, the change likewise in the sacrament is also true and not in a figure. ' [51]

Gardiner was well aware that the word 'transubstantiation' was neither in scripture nor in the early fathers. In this he readily concurred with the reformers. The difference centred on the *reality* of the change of the elements. In Catholic teaching this reality was in scripture and the fathers and was not a novelty of the papists.

'Albeit the word transubstantiation was first spoken of by public authority in that assembly of learned men of Christendom in a general council, where the bishop of Rome was present, yet the true matter signified by that word was older and believed before on the true understanding of Christ's words, and was in that council confessed, not for the authority of the bishop of Rome, but for the authority of truth, ... the true doctrine of Christ's mystery.' [52]

But neither was transubstantiation repugnant to reason. [53] The Catholic church had not put forth new and novel teaching. It was Cranmer and the reformers who were the innovators. According to Gardiner this new teaching contradicted the testimony of scripture and tradition.

'And therefore like as the teaching is new, to say it is an only figure or only signifieth: so the matter of signification must be newly devised, and new wine have new bottles, and be thoroughly new, after fifteen hundred and fifty

---

[51] *Ibid.,* p. 269.
[52] *Ibid.,* p. 239.
[53] *Ibid.,* pp. 251-252, 329.

years . . . to be newly erected and builded in Englishmen's hearts.' [54]

Gardiner expressed the traditional faith succinctly when he wrote,

> 'The true faith is that Christ's most precious body and blood is, by the might of his word and determination of his will, which he declareth by his word, in his holy supper present under form of bread and wine. The substance of which natures of bread and wine is converted into his most precious body and blood, as it is truly believed and taught in the catholic church.' [55]

Gardiner wrote with more sophistry than precision when he claimed this teaching to be similar to the doctrine of most protestants including Cranmer's close associates Martin Bucer and Peter Martyr. 'The faith of the real and substantial presence of Christ's body and blood in the sacrament is not the device of papists, or their faith only, as this author doth considerably slander it to be.' [56] Moreover Gardiner alleged that Cranmer's canons, his catechism and the 1549 Communion Service taught the Catholic doctrine of a true and real presence of Christ in the forms of bread and wine.

> 'A book set forth in the Archbishop of Canterbury's name, called a Catechism, willeth children to be taught that they receive with their bodily mouth the body and blood of Christ: which I allege, because it shall appear it as a teaching set forth among us of late, as hath been also, and is by the book of common prayer, being the most true Catholic doctrine on the substance of the sacrament.' [57]

Gardiner distinguished between a spiritual and a sacramental reception. Where he differed most trenchantly from the protestants was in his teaching that Christ could be received 'sacramentally only' and, therefore, sinfully by an ill-disposed person.

---

[54] *Ibid.*, p. 17.
[55] *Ibid.*, p. 51.
[56] *Ibid.*, p. 20.
[57] *Ibid.*, p. 55.

> 'Be the receivers worthy or unworthy, good or evil, the
> substance of Christ's sacrament is all one, as being God's
> work who worketh uniformly, so as it is neither better nor
> worse, but life or death of them that use it.' [58]

Moreover this real presence perdured unless and until a negli-
gent priest allowed the species to corrupt. As long as the
consecrated bread retained in the common estimation of men
the outward form of bread it remained in its inner substance
the glorified Christ. Reservation was commendable because it
enabled the priest to bring viaticum to the dying. Consecrated
bread 'was not wont to be reserved otherwise, but to be ready
for such as danger of death calleth for it'. [59]

Both Gardiner and Cranmer preferred that the people
communicate with the priest at the Lord's Supper. But Gardiner,
unlike Cranmer, tolerated masses in which only the priest
received.

> 'I never read anything of order in law or ceremony for-
> bidding the people to communicate with the priest, but
> all the old prayers and ceremonies sounded as the people
> did communicate with the priest. And when the people is
> prepared for, but then come not, but fearing and trembling
> forbear to come, that then the priest might not receive his
> part alone, the words of this epistle of Clement prove
> not.' [60]

Gardiner was neither a speculative nor an original theologian.
He was however well versed in the traditional faith of the
church. His doctrine of the real and true presence brought about
by the invisible Christ through the visible priest, a presence
which was natural and corporal yet mysterious, spiritual, and
beyond human understanding and which was aptly called transubstantiation because, through Christ's words spoken by the
priest, the inner reality was converted into Christ himself, a
presence which was effective before, during and after reception
— this was the faith of the Catholic church. Gardiner was the
principal spokesman for the adherents of the old faith during

[58] *Ibid.*, p. 68; cf. also pp. 26, 57, 70, 340.
[59] *Ibid.*, p. 59.
[60] *Ibid.*, p. 143.

the Henrician and Edwardian years, the crucial years in which Cranmer devised and put in use a new Ordinal. [61] Gardiner's teaching on priesthood was comprehensive. However, most of his writing on priesthood focused on the priest's power at the altar to consecrate bread and wine into the body and blood of Christ, a real and true presence which was an effective memorial and representation of Christ's all-sufficient sacrifice. [62]

Gardiner on Sacrificial Priesthood

In his Latin riposte to Cranmer's definitive *Answer* Gardiner reiterated traditional Catholic teaching on sacrifice. Through divine institution Christ's words at the Last Supper when pronounced with the proper intention by a priest were consecratory and sacrificial. The priest was a visible minister of Christ the high priest.

> 'For the increase of the dignity of our ministry God permits that these things which are his may be said of the minister. You learn from Ambrose that we ministers confect the body of Christ not by our words but by the divine words.' [63]

Gardiner adhered to the opinion, then under debate in the schools, that the Last Supper was a sacrifice. With the majority of theologians he taught that the Last Supper was a sacrifice in which Christ instituted the daily memorial of his unique sacrifice.

> 'The declaration of Christ's will in the Last Supper was for an offering of him to God the Father, assuring there

---

[61] Gardiner took his position of leadership in religion seriously. Cf. his objections to the Edwardine innovations, 'The Bishop of Winchester to Archbishop Cranmer relating to the Reformation of Religion', in John Strype, *Memorials of Archbishop Cranmer*, 3 Vols., Oxford, 1848, Vol. II, pp. 460-466; and 'Gardiner, Bishop of Winton, to the Duke of Somerset, Concerning the Book of Homilies and Erasmus', Paraphrase Englished, *Ibid.*, pp. 467-475. (Appendix).

[62] For Gardiner's arguments against the receptionist and 'merely commemorative' position of Hooper cf. *Responsio Venerabilium Sacerdotum*, Antwerp, 1564. In this posthumous publication Gardiner's own arguments are in the section entitled *Replicatio*.

[63] *Confutatio Cavillationum*, pp. 212-213; cf. 319.

his apostles of his will and determination, and by them all the world, that his body should be betrayed for them and us, and his precious blood shed for remission of sin, which his word he confirmed then with the gift of his precious body to be eaten and his precious blood to be drunken. In which mystery he declared His Body and Blood to be the very sacrifice of the world by him offered to God the Father.' [64]

Christ instituted the Mass as a visible *memorial* which applied the fruit of his death to later ages: 'the fruit of his death to pertain to us as well as to them.'

'Christ ordained this supper to be observed and continued for a memory of his coming; so as we saw not with our bodily eyes Christ's death and passion may in the celebration of the supper be most surely ascertained of this truth out of Christ's own mouth who still speaketh in the person of the minister of the church "This is my body that is betrayed for you: this is my blood which is shed for you in remission of sin": and therewith maketh his very body and his precious blood truly present to be taken of us, eaten, and drunken.' [65]

The mass therefore was an effective memorial, a representation, the very sacrifice of Calvary made effective in the present. The mass was propitiatory *not* because it added to Christ's sacrifice nor because it repeated that sacrifice but because the fruits of Christ's all-sufficient sacrifice were, through intercession, applied to the living and dead. In one of the last letters the prolific Gardiner ever wrote — when he was again in favour and Lord Chancellor of the realm — he directed Bishop Bonner to have masses offered for the late Pope Julius III as well as special prayers at mass for the blessing of a worthy successor. Through the mass therefore Christ's redemption was applied to the dead and, through petition, to temporal affairs.

'The king and the queen's majesty having certain knowledge of the death of the Pope's Holiness, thought good there should be as well solemn obsequies said for him

---

[64] 'Explicitation and Assertion', in *Writings and Disputations of Thomas Cranmer*, pp. 81-82.
[65] *Ibid.*, p. 82.

throughout the realm, as well these prayers which I send you herein enclosed, used at Mass times in all places at this time of vacation.' [66]

Christ's sacrifice was the one and only sacrifice satisfactory which redeemed the world. Christ was the one and only ransom who in his sacrifice appeased God. 'Christ the slain sacrifice and ransom of mankind who in appeasing the most justly deserved wrath of God hath declared the wholesome doctrine of obedience in his deeds.' [67] Gardiner reiterated this when Hooper charged that Catholic teaching added to Christ's sacrifice. 'When the Fathers say Christ to be offered and sacrificed by us, they understand a commemoration of his sacrifice which was done once by Christ on the cross.' [68] Against Cranmer he wrote that the mass was a *commemoration* of Calvary and therefore a sacrifice which did not *add* to Christ's sacrifice.

> 'This is agreed upon and by the scriptures plainly taught that the oblation and sacrifice of our Saviour Christ was and is a perfect work, once consummate in perfection without necessity of reiteration, as it was never taught to be reiterated, but a mere blasphemy to presuppose it. It is also in the Catholic teaching, grounded on the scripture, agreed that the same sacrifice once consummate was ordained by Christ's institution in his most holy supper to be in the church often remembered and showed forth. . .' [69]

Gardiner was reluctant to call the mass 'satisfactory' without explicit nuance lest the false impression be given that the priest's oblation added to Calvary. According to John Foxe's account of Gardiner's fateful sermon before King Edward VI on St Peter's Day, Gardiner maintained the traditional teaching that the mass was propitiatory and could be applied to the dead without thereby adding to Christ's sacrifice.

---

[66] 'Letter to Bonner', 10 April, 1555, in *Letters*, pp. 476-477.

[67] 'The Oration of True Obedience', in *Obedience in Church and State*, p. 77.

[68] *Responsio*, p. 77.

[69] 'Explicitation and Assertion', in *Writings and Disputations of Thomas Cranmer*, p. 344.

'When men add unto the mass an opinion of satisfaction or of a new redemption, then do they put it to another use than it was ordained for. I, that allow mass so well, and I, that allow praying for the dead (as indeed the dead are of Christian charity to be prayed for) yet can agree with the realm in that matter of putting down chantries.' [70]

Gardiner's reluctance to call the mass 'satisfactory' is an example of how concepts and even words can differ, both synchronically and diachronically, while intending the same mystery. [71] Scripture called Christ's sacrifice a ransom; Anselm called it satisfactory. Many medieval authors, while affirming the unicity of Christ's sacrifice, called the mass satisfactory because as a memorial it made Christ's sacrifice effective in the present. In his response to Cranmer's *Answer* Gardiner argued with a solicitor's acumen,

'Since the thing which is truly contained in the sacrament is made the same body which hung on the cross; the same always was, is, and will be satisfaction for the sins of the whole world. And although no-one says the sacrament is satisfaction in this sense; nevertheless we profess that in the sacrament is truly present the body of Christ which satisfied for the sins of the world.' [72]

There was one mediator, the heavenly high priest Jesus Christ. Priests are mediators because they participate in Christ's mediation. Writing against John Hooper, Gardiner argued, 'Every prayer of the church terminates with the words 'through Christ Our Lord' that the power of mediation may be retained in Christ through whom alone there is access to the Father.' [73]

In defending Catholic doctrine that the mass was propitiatory Gardiner explained that the fruits of Calvary were not automatically efficacious independently of the dispositions of the persons participating.

---

[70] John Foxe, *Acts and Monuments,* Vol. VI, pp. 89-90.

[71] L. Malavez, 'L'invariant et le divers dans le langage de la foi', *Nouvelle Revue Theologique,* April, 1973, pp. 353-365, esp. pp. 353-355.

[72] *Confutatio Cavillationum,* p. 148; cf. 'Explicitation and Assertion', in *Writings and Disputations of Thomas Cranmer,* pp. 81, 361.

[73] *Responsio,* p. 108; cf. 'Explicitation and Assertion', in *Writings and Disputations of Thomas Cranmer,* p. 234.

> 'The Catholic doctrine teacheth not the daily sacrifice of
> Christ's most precious body and blood to be an iteration
> of the once perfected sacrifice on the cross... The daily
> offering is propitiatory also, but not in that degree of
> propitiation, as for redemption, regeneration or remission
> of deadly sin, which was once purchased, and by force
> thereof is in the sacraments ministered; but for the increase
> of God's favour, the mitigation of God's displeasure,
> provoked by our infirmities, the subduing of temptation
> and the perfection of virtue in us.' [74]

Catholic priests, therefore, were offerers of a representative
memorial of Christ's one sacrifice. Only because Christ's sacrifice was effective in the present could the mass be called satisfactory. The action of the priest *added* nothing to Christ's
sacrifice.

> 'To call the daily offering a "sacrifice satisfactory" must
> have an understanding that signifieth not the action of the
> priest, but the presence of Christ's most precious body
> and blood, the very sacrifice of the world once perfectly
> offered being propitiatory and satisfactory for all the
> world ... otherwise the daily action in respect of the priest
> cannot be called satisfactory, and it is a word indeed that
> soundeth not well so placed, although it might be saved
> by a signification.' [75]

In Catholic teaching the mass in representation and memorial
was the same propitiatory sacrifice as Calvary. Gardiner stated
that the priest did not preside over a memorial which was
merely commemorative and which merely reminded those present
of their redemption. Rather, in Catholic teaching the daily
memorial made that redemption effective in the present.

> 'When the minister pronounceth Christ's words, as spoken
> of his mouth, it is to be believed, that Christ doeth now,
> as he did then. And it is to be noted that although in the
> sacrament of baptism the minister saith "I baptize thee",
> yet in the celebration of his supper the words be spoken
> in Christ's person, as saying himself "This is my body
> that is broken for you", which is unto us not only a

---

[74] *Ibid.*, p. 360.
[75] *Ibid.*, p. 361.

> memory, but an effectual memory, with the very presence
> of Christ's body and blood, our very sacrifice: who doing
> now, as he did then, offereth himself to his Father as he
> did then, not to renew that offering as though it were
> imperfect, but continually to refresh us that daily fall and
> decay.' [76]

Because the mass makes Christ's sacrifice effective in the present
and because men sin daily Gardiner defended daily masses.
Gardiner's teaching about the application of the mass to daily
sins was orthodox because of his insistence that Christ's sacrifice was all-sufficient for all sins, original and actual. Yet in
his defence of daily masses Gardiner was approximating that
'false teaching' alleged by the reformers whereby Catholics
taught that Calvary satisfied for original, the mass for daily
sins. [77] In his exposition of Peter Lombard Gardiner expressed
traditional and orthodox Catholic doctrine; but in his repeated
connection between the mass and daily sins Gardiner was not
at his best.

> 'The visible church hath priests in ministry that offer daily
> Christ's most precious body and blood in mystery ... this
> daily offering by the priest is daily offered for sin, not for
> any imperfection in the first offering, but because we daily
> fall.' [78]

Christ's all-sufficient sacrifice was a sacrifice which included
his passion and death. The mass was a memorial of Christ's
sacrifice — but without bloodshed. [79] Cranmer and the reformers,
who alleged that every sacrifice meant the death of the victim
offered, occasionally distorted Catholic teaching as if traditional
teaching was that Christ was daily slain on the altar. Neither the
Council of Trent nor subsequent Catholic teaching has defined
just *what* precisely a sacrifice is and *how* the mass is a sacrifice.
Gardiner argued correctly that,

---

[76] *Ibid.*, p. 83; cf. pp. 344, 359.
[77] Francis Clark, *Eucharistic Sacrifice and the Reformation,* pp. 469-504.
[78] 'Explicitation and Assertion', in *Writings and Disputations of Thomas
Cranmer,* p. 358.
[79] *Confutatio Cavillationum,* p. 6.

'This sacrifice done after the order of Melchisidech, Christ's death is not iterate, but a memory daily renewed of that death, so as Christ's offering on the cross once done and consummate to finish all sacrifices after the order of Aaron is now only remembered according to Christ's institution, but in such wise as the same body is offered daily on the altar, that was once offered on the altar of the cross; but the same manner of offering is not daily that was on the altar of the cross, for the daily offering is without bloodshed, and is termed so to signify that bloodshedding once done to be sufficient.' [86]

Gardiner's exegesis went beyond the evidence when he compared Catholic priests to the delegates and elders of the Pastoral epistles. For there is no clear evidence in scripture that these men presided at the eucharist. [81] However, Gardiner's arguments that priests were teachers, leaders and sanctifiers are a contemporary witness to the faith. Christian priesthood differed from hereditary priesthood.

'The priesthood of Christ endeth not in him to go to another by succession, as in the tribe of Levi, where there was among mortal men succession in the office of priesthood; but Christ liveth ever, and therefore is a perpetual everlasting priest, by whose authority priesthood is now in this visible church, as St Paul ordered to Timothy and Titus, and other places also confirm, which priests, visible ministers to our invisible priest, offer the daily sacrifice in Christ's church; that is to say, with the very presence of God's omnipotency wrought, of the most precious body and blood of our Saviour Christ, showing forth Christ's death, and celebrating the memory of his supper and death according to Christ's institution, so with daily oblation and sacrifice of the self same sacrifice to kindle in us a thankful remembrance of all Christ's benefits unto us.' [82]

---

[80] 'Explicitation and Assertion', in *Writings and Disputations of Thomas Cranmer,* p. 364.

[81] Aelred Cody, 'Foundation of the Church', *Theological Studies,* March, 1973, pp. 3-19, esp. pp. 3-11.

[82] 'Explicitation and Assertion', in *Writings and Disputations of Thomas Cranmer,* p. 363.

Gardiner taught that Christ's sacrifice is 'our very only sacrifice'. [83] In Gardiner's words,

> '... by Christ's own mouth we be ascertained of his most glorious death and passion, and the selfsame body that suffered, delivered unto us in mystery, to be eaten of us, and therefore so to be worshipped, and acknowledged of us as our very only sacrifice, in whom, by whom, and for whom our gifts and sacrifices be acceptable and no otherwise.' [84]

Conclusion

Stephen Gardiner of Winchester was the acknowledged spokesman for the Henrician 'Catholic' party during the years of the Henrician and Edwardine reformation. In the last months of his life — after renewing his Roman allegiance — he was one of the principal spokesmen of those who endorsed the Marian reaction.

Gardiner's concept of priesthood was the same as that reflected in the Sarum pontifical. Together they reflect the traditional belief of the church. [85] Two cautions are in order, however, when assessing Gardiner. First, he was not a professional theologian but a trained lawyer and bishop of the church with a good knowledge of theology. [86] Secondly, we have concentrated — as indeed Gardiner himself concentrated — on the priest's role at the eucharist because it was the point at issue in the sixteenth century. However, neither Gadiner nor the mainstream of Catholic theology limited priesthood to this role. In fact Gardiner, despite his belief in purgatory and masses for

---

[83] *Agreement On The Eucharist, The Windsor Statement of the Anglican/Roman Catholic International Commission,* December 31st, 1971, Alan Clark, ed., London, 1972, pp. 6-10, esp. p. 8.

[84] 'Explicitation and Assertion', in *Writings and Disputations of Thomas Cranmer,* pp. 83-84.

[85] H. Francis Davis, 'The Reformers and the Eucharist', in *Clergy Review,* July, 1959, pp. 407-417.

[86] Gordon Rupp, 'Foreward' in Peter Brooks, *Thomas Cranmer's Doctrine Of The Eucharist,* London, 1965, p. vii.

the dead, approved of the suppression of chantries when the resident priests were merely offerers of *scala coeli* masses. [87]

In Gardiner's (and traditional Catholic) teaching the mass was not a 'work' which merited salvation or supplemented Christ's sacrifice. The redemptive act of Christ was sufficient for the justification of all men *including* those who sin daily between the Ascension and parousia. The mass was a memorial of Calvary and *not* a daily slaying of Christ.

Gardiner seemingly contended that bishops and priests ordained with Cranmer's Ordinals were still laymen. But it is not clear *why* he held this. The fragmentary evidence available inclines this writer to believe that Gardiner held these orders void because Cranmer omitted ceremonies which signified the priest's power to consecrate and offer the eucharist.

For Gardiner the ministry was a comprehensive service that reached its climax at the altar but which was not limited to cult. He transmitted traditional teaching that the hierarchy were leaders who enjoyed the awesome power to excommunicate heretics and schismatics. The bishop enjoyed powers which priests did not have — such as the powers to consecrate and ordain, to confirm, to bless and reconcile churches, and to bless chrism, vestments, chalices, cemeteries etc. [88] Both bishops and priests reconciled sinners to Christ and the church in the sacrament of penance, both administered extreme unction and presided at marriages and funerals. Both were ministers of the *word* as well as of the sacraments.

Significantly Gardiner taught that ordained ministers should be men of outstanding virtue. They were to pray for those they served. Although Gardiner himself never lost his love for affluence and pomp he transmitted faithfully the teaching that ministers were to be an example of virtue to their people. The virtue which Gardiner stressed the most was chastity.

---

[87] John Foxe, *Acts and Monuments*, Vol. VI, pp. 89-91.
[88] For the theory of parity of ministers held by the reformers cf. J.L. Ainslee, *The Doctrine of Ministerial Order in the Reformed Churches of the Sixteenth and Seventeenth Centuries*, Edinburgh, 1940, pp. 91-123.

When Cranmer attacked Gardiner's teaching on the priest-hood he was protesting against something more than late medieval distortions, abuses, superstitions and the practical mass system. [89] In denying the minister's power to consecrate and offer the eucharist he was repudiating part of the traditional teaching on priesthood of which Gardiner was in his time the principal spokesman in England.

---

[89] That late medieval eucharistic theology of the mass was substantially sound and that Gardiner was expressing traditional teaching is well argued by H. Francis Davis, 'The Reformers and the Eucharist', in *The Clergy Review*, July, 1959, pp. 407-417, esp. pp. 415-417.

CHAPTER III

Thomas Cranmer

'The roots of the weeds, is the popish doctrine of transubstantiation, of the real presence of Christ's flesh and
blood in the sacrament of the altar (as they call it), and
of the sacrifice and oblation of Christ made by the priest,
for the salvation of the quick and the dead.'

Thomas Cranmer

We have studied sixteenth century belief in priesthood as that
belief was reflected in the Sarum pontifical and in the writings
of Stephen Gardiner. Thomas Cranmer broke with that traditional belief and expressed his reformed ideas in a new Ordinal.
But first a few words about Cranmer himself.

The primary author of the Anglican Ordinal was born in
1489 at Aslockton, Nottinghamshire. Cranmer's formal education
began at the age of seven — and he was a scholar for the rest of
his life. At the age of fourteen he entered Jesus College, Cambridge, where he eventually became a Fellow. When he was
twenty-five he resigned his fellowship to marry. Within less
than a year his wife had died and Cranmer was readmitted to
his fellowship, became a priest, a reader in Divinity, a licensed
university preacher and a methodical and independent student
of scripture, the early church, the fathers, medieval authors, and
the contemporary writings of the continental reformers which
were circulating at Cambridge.

In 1529 Cranmer told Stephen Gardiner and Edward Fox, both of whom were in the entourage of Henry VIII, that the King's petitions for the nullity of his first marriage should be settled not in ecclesiastical courts but in the universities. He was summoned to London where he expressed his conviction that the King's first marriage, to his late brother's wife, was invalid.

In 1530 he was a royal envoy to the continent where, in German and Italian lands, he tried to persuade the continental universities to back the King's case. In 1532, as ambassador to Charles V, he became a personal friend of several Lutheran reformers and married the niece of Osiander.

In 1533 Cranmer was recalled to England to succeed Warham as Archbishop of Canterbury. At his consecration he read aloud a carefully worded 'protestation' qualifying his oath of obedience to the Pope. [1] As primate he promptly ruled that, despite the delaying tactics of the Pope, Henry was free to take Anne Boleyn as his queen.

Although he himself was an independent thinker Cranmer condemned John Frith in 1533 for denying the real presence and the efficacy of masses for the dead. In the same year, however, he licensed Hugh Latimer to preach throughout the land — and Latimer was notorious for his liberal views.

In a Lenten sermon in 1535 Cranmer attacked several abuses of the contemporary mass system and defended the royal confiscation of certain chantries. Yet in 1536 he supported legislation in favour of the real presence, private masses and masses for the dead. [2]

In 1538 we notice in Cranmer a definite, albeit typically independent, sympathy for at least some of the thoughts of the reformers. In that year he sent three anabaptists to the stake for

---

[1] Jasper Ridley, *Thomas Cranmer*, Oxford, 1962, pp. 55-57; cf. Edward Carpenter, 'Thomas Cranmer, Sensitive Theologian', in *Cantuar, The Archbishops in their Office*, London, 1971, pp. 134-135.

[2] Ridley, *Cranmer*, p. 165.

E

denying the real presence,[3] and condemned John Lambert.[4] But in an interesting letter to Thomas Cromwell about one Adam Damplip Cranmer referred to transubstantiation as an 'opinion'. 'He saith that the controversy between him and the Prior was because he confuted the opinion of the transubstantiation, and therein I think he taught but the truth.'[5]

However, when Six 'Catholic' articles were passed in 1539 endorsing transubstantiation and clerical celibacy Cranmer acquiesced. He enforced the legislation and quietly sent his wife to Germany for four years.[6] He argued in the House of Lords that confession to a priest, while tolerable, was not of divine law,[7] yet in obedience to the King, he upheld articles defending transubstantiation and private masses.[8] He condemned a man named Barnes for denying doctrines which Cranmer himself was beginning to question — transubstantiation, purgatory, and the efficacy of masses for the dead,[9] and with the promulgation of the theologically conservative 'King's Book' in 1543 accepted as law the doctrines of the real presence, transubstantiation, and private confession.[10] Yet in 1545, he again supported the royal suppression of certain chantries.

What has often appeared as vacillation in Cranmer was in fact consistent with his belief in royal supremacy. The King's wish was the archbishop's command even when the former reversed himself for amorous or political reasons. Cranmer, however, was no faceless courtier. From 1545 until his own martyrdom a decade later Cranmer, in his mature years and at

---

[3] 'Cranmer to Cromwell, 8-10 October, 1538', in *Miscellaneous Writings and Letters of Thomas Cranmer,* John Edmund Cox, ed., (Parker Society), Cambridge, 1846, pp. 381-384; 'Cranmer to Cromwell, 11 January, 1539', *Ibid.,* pp. 387-388.

[4] Ridley, *Cranmer,* p. 176.

[5] 'Cranmer to Cromwell, 24 July 1538', in *Miscellaneous Writings,* p. 317; cf. John Foxe, *Acts and Monuments,* Vol. V, p. 501.

[6] Ridley, *Cranmer,* p. 178.

[7] *Ibid.,* p. 181.

[8] Gordon Rupp, *Six Makers of English Religion,* 1500-1700, Liverpool, 1964, p. 41.

[9] Ridley, *Cranmer,* p. 206.

[10] *Ibid.,* pp. 239-240.

the peak of his powers, was consistently moderate in theology and, as an independent scholar, developed his own ideas without adherence to any particular party.

The year 1546 was important for Cranmer's doctrine on priesthood and, therefore, on the subsequent history of Anglican ministry. In that year he engaged in lengthy and learned conversations with Nicholas Ridley about the doctrine of the eucharist. He had already questioned transubstantiation; sometime after his discussions with Ridley he no longer believed in the traditional doctrine of a real and special presence of Christ in the eucharist through a mysterious change in the sacramental elements. [11]

Cranmer's independence and moderation appeared in 1547 when Henry VIII died. The archbishop, although he had his own ideas on priesthood which differed from the traditional belief, disapproved of disrespect to priests and to irrational image smashing. [12] He permitted books by the reformers to circulate, recommended freedom for priests to marry, and advocated communion under both species; but in his visitation injunctions he rejected innovations unless they were approved by the young King. [13] In December Cranmer prepared a series of pointed questions to be answered by himself and other bishops on abuses connected with the eucharist. [14] As we shall see his own answers reflect his mature doctrine on priesthood and therefore on the doctrine of the forthcoming new Ordinal.

---

[11] *The Works of Bishop Ridley,* Henry Christmas, ed., (Parker Society) Cambridge, 1841, p. 407; cf. also Thomas Cranmer, 'The Answer to Smith's Preface', in *Writings and Disputations of Thomas Cranmer Relative to the Sacrament of the Lord's Supper,* p. 374.

[12] Ridley, *Cranmer,* pp. 363-364. Cranmer was less than enthusiastic about the Edwardine confiscation of chantries, not because he still held the traditional doctrine about masses for the dead but because he objected to the greed and materialism endemic in the English confiscation of church property. Cf. Maurice Powicke, *The Reformation in England,* London, 1965, p. 35.

[13] Homilies, in *Miscellaneous Writings,* pp. 128-149.

[14] Gilbert Burnet, *The History of the Reformation of the Church of England,* N. Pocock ed., Oxford, 1865, Vol. V, pp. 197-217. Burnet seems to reproduce accurately these questions and Cranmer's answers.

In 1548 the archbishop curtailed some ceremonies and strictly enforced the licensing of preachers. In March he issued his vernacular Order of the Communion, for insertion into the Latin Mass, in which communicants were permitted to confess grave sins to *God* and, in cases of reconsecration, priests were forbidden to elevate the newly consecrated elements. [15] Also in 1548 Cranmer translated into English Justus Jonas' catechism in such a way as to imply a receptionist presence of Christ in the eucharist. In December, in the House of Lords, he publicly defended a receptionist doctrine of the presence distinguishing between eating 'the sacrament' and dwelling in the Body of Christ. 'They be twoo things to eate the Sacrament and to eate the bodie of Christ. The eating of the bodie is to dwell in Christ, and this may be thoo a man never taste the Sacrament.' [16] Meanwhile he was the principal architect of a new Communion Service, promulgated on Whitsun, 1549, which reflected his belief that the Lord's Supper was an oblation of 'ourselves, our souls and bodies; our praise and thanksgiving.' [17] After the fall of Somerset and the rise of Warwick Cranmer required even *bishops* to be licensed to preach — and they were to preach a receptionist doctrine of the eucharist. [18] In 1550 the new Ordinal, of which Cranmer was the primary author, appeared; in the Ordinal the Sarum pontifical was considerably modified by the elimination of almost all medieval additions which signified the priest's power to offer sacrifice. [19] Also in 1550, most remaining altars, chantries and statues were removed, communion tables erected, and Cranmer's *Defence* against the eucharistic teaching of Gardiner (and the Roman church)

[15] G.J. Cuming, *A History of Anglican Liturgies,* Glasgow, 1969, pp. 364-366.
[16] J.T. Tomlinson, *The Great Parliamentary Debate in 1548 on the Lord's Supper,* London, n.d., pp. 27-53, esp. pp. 27-28.
[17] Edward P. Echlin, *The Anglican Eucharist in Ecumenical Perspective,* pp. 9-46.
[18] 'Hooper to Bullinger, 27 December, 1549', in *Original Letters Relative to the English Reformation,* Hastings Robinson, ed., 2 Vols., Parker Society, Cambridge, 1842-1845, Vol. I, pp. 71-72: 'Hooper to Bullinger, 5 February, 1550', *Ibid.,* p. 76.
[19] *The First Prayer Book of King Edward VI,* London, n.d., pp. 281-290.

published. In 1551 Cranmer answered Gardiner's prompt reply with his final, definitive (and polemical) *Answer*, a work in which he repeated the arguments of his *Defence* and answered passage by passage Gardiner's *Explicitation and Assertion.*

In 1552 Cranmer's final Communion Service and Ordinal appeared in which he further deleted references to sacrificial priesthood. The archbishop, however, remained independent and moderate. His writings and liturgies never went far enough to satisfy the more extreme English reformers and their continental sympathizers. He insisted against John Knox that communion should be received kneeling. [20] He drew up a draft revision of church law in which, even in a state-church, bishops were guardians against heresy with the power to excommunicate. [21] Cranmer also prepared forty-five articles of religion for a moderate English church. The articles, reduced to forty-two, were circulated briefly before the death of Edward. Cranmer at first supported the Lady Jane Grey succession. When the coup proved abortive he promised obedience to Mary Tudor.

Soon after Mary's triumphant accession and Gardiner's return to the halls of power its was rumoured in the southeast that the Archbishop of Canterbury had reintroduced the Catholic mass — and therefore priesthood — into his diocese. In one of the most courageous acts of his life the Archbishop vehemently repudiated the rumour in a forthright 'Declaration' against the mass, realizing that his action meant at least imprisonment and possibly death for heresy. [22] Indeed Cranmer went to the tower on 14 September, 1553.

Thereafter Cranmer was subjected to three different 'trials', in all of which he was prosecuted, at least in part, for his teaching on the eucharist. In November, 1553, he was convicted of treason. In March, 1554, he was compelled to engage in a public debate at Oxford with the papal party on the doctrines

---

[20] Echlin, *The Anglican Eucharist in Ecumenical Perspective*, pp. 85-88.

[21] Powicke, *The Reformation in England*, pp. 37-39; 61-62.

[22] Rupp, *Six Makers of English Religion*, p. 47; cf. also Francis Proctor and Walter Frere, *A New History of the Book of Common Prayer*, pp. 91-93.

of transubstantiation, the real presence, and the sacrificial nature of the mass. He was convicted, with Latimer and Ridley, for heresy. However, he still had seventeen months of life remaining in Oxford's Bocardo before his final trial and death. His unfinished response to Gardiner's *Confutatio Cavillationum* was in part confiscated and in part lost through the negligence of John Foxe. While in prison he also began a tract against the traditional arguments on eucharist and priesthood put forth at 'the grey towers of Durham' by Cuthbert Tunstall during the latter's house arrest under Edward VI, but this response was likewise unfinished, confiscated, and lost forever. [23] In a golden Oxford September, 1555, Cranmer was tried yet again, this time by papal commissioners, for heresy. Once again his later teachings on eucharist and priesthood were a major indictment against him, and once again he was condemned. This meant degradation, humiliation, and the terrible anticipation of death above the faggots. The months dragged on, Latimer and especially Ridley died in agony. Cranmer, in the final weeks of his life, issued several retractions of his mature teaching on the eucharist. A host of authors have debated these *volte face* documents to which the fearful, tormented and aging convict added his signature. [24]

Suffice to say here that Cranmer's *ultimate* recantation, given in St Mary's church moments before his death, in which he retracted his previous recantations, is the one final testament that truly represents Thomas Cranmer's teaching on eucharist and priesthood. 'And as for the Sacrament, I believe as I have taught in my book against the bishop of Winchester.' [25] The

---

[23] Cuthbert Tunstall, *De Veritate Corporis et Sanguinis Domini Nostri Jesu Christi,* Paris, 1554.

[24] Cf. for example W. Whiston, *An Inquiry into the Evidence of Archbishop Cranmer's Recantation,* London, 1736; H.J. Todd, *A Reply to Dr Lingard's Vindication of His History of England as far as respects Archbishop Cranmer,* London, 1827; Philobiblon Society, *Bishop Cranmer's Recantacyons,* Vol. XV, London, 1874; A.J. Mason, *Thomas Cranmer,* London, 1898; A.F. Pollard, *Thomas Cranmer and the English Reformation, 1489-1556,* London, 1926 ed.; Ridley, *Thomas Cranmer,* esp. pp. 383-411.

[25] Quoted in Ridley, *Thomas Cranmer,* p. 407.

Answer to Gardiner best reveals Cranmer's reformed doctrine and therefore the doctrine he expressed liturgically in the Anglican Ordinal.

Ministers of Word and Sacrament

John Strype observed that Cranmer's final eucharistic tract is of singular value because it was the culmination of a lifetime of reading and study. Strype's words are worth repeating.

'His discourse, wherein he stated the Doctrine of the Sacrament in five Books, must especially be remembered. Which he wrote on purpose for the public instruction of the Church of England. And it is the more to be valued, as being writ by him in his mature Age, after all his great Readings and Studies, and most diligent and serious perusals of all the Ecclesiastical Writers; whereby he became thoroughly acquainted with their Judgments and Opinions in that Doctrine. And in it are contained his last and ripest Thoughts on that Argument. This Book displayeth the great Weakness of that distinguishing Doctrine of the Church of Rome, that asserts Transubstantiation.' [26]

Cranmer's independent mind sifted a variety of sources. [27] He studied not only scripture and the fathers but also the medieval writers, contemporary German and Swiss reformers, and the writings of Catholics such as Gardiner, Pole, Smith and Tunstall. [28]

From his years as a reader at Cambridge until the reign of Edward VI Cranmer's thought was in a state of transition from acceptance of Roman teaching, including the 'opinion' of transubstantiation, to his final, mature doctrine. In his reading and study he compiled *florilegia* from a surprisingly wide variety of sources. As Peter Brooks remarks,

---

[26] John Strype, *Memorials of the Most Reverend Father in God, Thomas Cranmer,* 3 Vols., London, 1644 edition, Vol. III, p. 395.

[27] C.W. Dugmore, *The Mass and the English Reformers,* London, 1958, p. vii.

[28] G.W. Bromiley has interesting observations on Cranmer's study of scripture and the fathers in *Thomas Cranmer Theologian,* London, 1956, pp. 23-30.

'The fact that such *florilegia* were collected from a Real
Presence point of view, and include passages taken from
the writings of Luther and other Continental Reformers,
shows both that their owner had no parochial suspicion of
those divines, and also suggests that he felt Scripture,
Fathers and Reformers to be not at all antithetical.' [29]

Brooks also observes that 'as late as autumn 1548 Cranmer was
not publically known to favour either Roman or Swiss views
on the sacrament.' [30] This does not mean Cranmer's views were
not settled. After 1548, for Cranmer it was mainly a matter of
expressing his thoughts in his liturgies and polemical writings. [31]
He was not 'Roman', 'German' or 'Swiss'; he was Cranmer, an
independent, discreet and moderate scholar. Cranmer adopted
major features of reformed thought; but he endeavoured to
transcend divisive details that put the reformers at odds among
themselves. No statement ever made by Cranmer better describes
the independent bent of his mind than his remark to Joachim
Vadian in 1537, 'I have seen almost everything that has been
written or published either by Oecolampadius or Zwinglius, and
*I have come to the conclusion that the writings of every man
should be read with discrimination.*' [32] Cranmer's doctrine was
grounded in scripture. But he interpreted scripture with the
assistance of authors of past and present. As a man of his epoch
he was, like any theologian of any epoch, limited by the exegetical science available to his age. [33] His teaching on the develop-

[29] Peter Brooks, *Thomas Cranmer's Doctrine on the Eucharist,* London,
1965, p. 11.

[30] *Ibid.,* p. 10.

[31] Echlin, *The Anglican Eucharist in Ecumenical Perspective,* pp. 21-
22; Gregory Dix in *The Shape of the Liturgy,* London, 1945, pp.
646, 656 is a bit simplistic in saying Cranmer's doctrine was in-
distinguishable from that of Zwingli; cf. also Dix, 'Dixit Cranmer
et Non Timuit', in *The Church Quarterly Review,* January-March,
pp. 145-176; C.C. Richardson, *Zwingli and Cranmer on the Eucharist,* Evanston, 1949, p. 48; Edward Carpenter, *Cantuar, The Archbishops in their Office,* pp. 138-139.

[32] 'Cranmer to Joachim Vadian, 1537', in *Original Letters,* Vol. I,
p. 13 (Italics added).

[33] Raymond A. Brown, 'The Current Crisis of Theology As It Affects
the Teaching of Catholic Doctrine', *The National Catholic Reporter,*
May 11, 1973, pp. 9-10; 15-16.

ment of the mono-episcopate, for example, traces this development to an earlier period than does modern Roman Catholic
scholarship. In his recourse to reformed exegesis he embraced
those interpretations which he thought interpreted the word of
God — and he eschewed what seemed novel or divisive. Despite
the strain under which he laboured in his final months at
Oxford the following summary of his theological method seems
accurate.

> 'In the assertions of the church and of religion, trifling and
> new-fangled novelties of words, so much as may be, are
> to be eschewed, whereof riseth nothing but contention and
> brawling about words; and we must follow, so much as we
> may, the manner of speaking of the scripture.' [34]

In 1540 Cranmer made some interesting observations 'concerning
the sacraments and the power of bishops and priests' which
merit some attention. At that time he was attempting to reconcile the complications endemic in a royal supremacy, now
independent of the Roman bishop, with the ordering of ministers.
Some of his more radical observations of 1540 were modified
by the time he composed his Ordinal. [35] Others were definitive.
In still others he touched brilliantly on the complex development of a Christian priesthood. [36] His touch, however, was
unsure; partly because of his administrative duties and partly
because of the as yet undiscovered findings of post-reformation
scholarship. [37]

   In 1540 Cranmer argued that princes supervised not only
the civil service but also the ministry of the word and care of
souls. Princes were empowered to elect, assign and appoint *all*
ministers, civil and ecclesiastical, in their realms. Ordination and
installation ceremonies were comely and for good order but not

---

[34] 'An Explicitation of Cranmer Upon the Aforesaid Conclusions
  Exhibited in Writing', Disputations at Oxford, in *Writings and
  Disputations Relative to the Lord's Supper*, p. 395.
[35] Ridley, *Thomas Cranmer,* pp. 208-212; 260.
[36] Jean Tillard, *What Priesthood Has the Ministry,* Bramcote, 1973,
  esp. pp. 20-28.
[37] *Ibid.*

necessary. [38] Moreover, no special grace was transmitted in ordination,

> 'In the admission of many of these officers be divers comely ceremonies and solemnities used, which be not of necessity, but only for a good order and seemly fasion: for if such offices and ministrations were committed without such solemnity, they were nevertheless truly committed. And there is no more promise of God, that grace is given in the committing of the ecclesiastical office, than it is in the committing of the civil office.' [39]

Cranmer demonstrated a surprisingly keen insight into pristine church ordering when he observed that in apostolic times God's people recognized as their ministers those men who came forward, under the Spirit's guidance, as leaders with special gifts of wisdom and council — and that in emergency situations such recognition was sufficient for authentic ordering. [40]

> 'In the apostles' time, when there was no christian princes, by whose authority ministers of God's word might be appointed, nor sins by the sword corrected, there was no remedy then for the correction of vice, or appointing of ministers, but only the consent of christian multitude among themselves, by an uniform consent to follow the advice and persuasion of such persons whom God had most endued with the spirit of counsel and wisdom.' [41]

Cranmer seconded Jerome's theory of an original parity of ministers. The first *episcopoi* and 'priests' were one office. 'The bishops and priests were at one time, and were not two things, but both one office in the beginning of Christ's religion.' [42] Soon, however, the bishop was made a *primus inter pares* in any one

---

[38] 'Questions and Answers Concerning the Sacraments' in *Miscellaneous Writings*, p. 116; cf. also John Strype, *Memorials*, 1848 edition, Vol. I, pp. 417-423.

[39] 'Questions and Answers Concerning the Sacraments', in *Miscellaneous Writings*, p. 116.

[40] Edward P. Echlin, 'Towards a Contemporary Appropriation of Apostolicae Curae', *The Ampleforth Journal*, July, 1972, pp. 8-30; esp. pp. 17-23.

[41] 'Questions and Answers Concerning the Sacraments', in *Miscellaneous Writings*, p. 116.

[42] *Ibid.*, p. 117.

of four ways: through episcopal consecration, through appointment by kings, through appointment by governors, or through recognition by the people of those put forward as their leaders.

'A bishop may make a priest by the scripture, and so may princes and governors also, and that by the authority of God committed to them, and the people also by their election: for as we read that bishops have done it, so christian emperors and princes usually have done it; and the people, before christian princes were, commonly did elect their bishops and priests.' [43]

Cranmer used the argument from silence — always a perilous methodology — and he disregarded some evidence for ordering in the 'early Catholic' writings when he asserted that in the New Testament no consecration of a 'bishop' or 'priest' was necessary. 'In the New Testament he that is appointed to be a bishop or a priest, needeth no consecration by the scripture; for election or appointing thereto is sufficient. [44] Therefore in infidel lands and in regions where the hierarchy had died out the 'godly prince' was empowered to ordain a native clergy. Cranmer conceded that bishops and priests enjoyed a special power to excommunicate and to hear private confessions — but neither power was of divine law.

'A bishop or a priest by the scripture is neither commanded nor forbidden to excommunicate, but where the laws of any region giveth him authority to excommunicate, there they ought to use the same in such crimes as the laws have such authority in; and where the laws of the region forbiddeth them, there they have none authority at all: and they that be no priests may also excommunicate, if the law allow them thereunto.' [45]

As for the priest's power of anointing, 'Unction of the sick with oil to remit venial sins, as it is now used, is not spoken of in the scripture, nor in any ancient author.' [46]

Fifteen years later Cranmer argued that he had professed but two successive doctrines on the eucharist — the Roman one and, after 1546, his definitive one articulated in his published

---

[43] *Ibid.*
[44] *Ibid.*

[45] *Ibid.*
[46] *Ibid.*

Answer to Gardiner. Correlatively, his doctrine on priesthood underwent similar development before the publication of his Ordinal in 1550. In 1540 his thoughts were still in transition as he himself conceded in the conclusion to his 1540 questions and answers concerning the sacraments. 'This is mine opinion and sentence at this present, which I do not temerariously define, and do remit the judgment thereof wholly unto your majesty.' [47]

In 1548, however, Cranmer was answering questions concerning the sacraments in a less tentative manner. In that year he responded to his own catena of queries of important bishops and divines, 'concerning some abuses of the mass'. His crisp answers, especially when compared with the responses of the conservative Tunstall of Durham, demonstrate clearly that, for Cranmer, the priest had no power to offer sacrifice.

To his question, 'Whether the sacrament of the altar was instituted to be received of one man for another, or to be received of every man for himself?' Cranmer replied, 'The sacrament of the altar was not instituted to be received of one man for another, but to be received of every man for himself.' This implied that the hallowed practice of applying the eucharistic memorial by the priest for other persons, present or absent, was contrary to the institution of Christ. Tunstall conceded that 'the sacrament of the altar was instituted, to be received of every man by himself, to make him a member of Christ's mystical body, and to knit and unite him to Christ our head.' [48] Cranmer's break with traditional teaching appears more vividly in the answers to the second question, 'Whether the receiving of the said sacrament of one man, do avail and profit any other?' Cranmer replied, 'the receiving of the said sacrament by one man doth avail and profit only him that receiveth the same.' Tunstall, however, referring to the Pauline writings,

---

[47] *Ibid.*

[48] 'Queries put concerning some abuses of the mass; with the answers made by many bishops and divines to them', in Gilbert Burnet, *The History of the Reformation of the Church of England,* Vol. V, pp. 197-215. The questions and answers quoted in the subsequent pages are taken from the collection of primary sources edited by Pocock.

defended the application of the priest's communion to other
Christians.

> 'The receiving of the sacrament of one man doth profit
> another, as the health and good-liking of one member,
> doth in part strengthen the body, and other members of the
> same: for St Paule saith, *Multi unum corpus sumus in
> Christo, singuli autem alter alterius membra, Rom. 12 et
> 1 Cor. 12. Si gaudet unum membrum, congaudent omnia
> membra.*'

The next question was more pointed: 'What is the oblation and
sacrifice of Christ in the mass?' Significantly, Cranmer acknowledged that the eucharist is a memory and representation of the
one Christian sacrifice. But for Cranmer a sacrament did not
contain what it signified; the representation and memorial was
manward, 'to men', and not with and to God. The tragedy is
that Cranmer and the representatives of the old faith were
enmeshed in a polemical atmosphere coloured by superstitious
theories of sacrifice, the abuses of the current stipendary system,
and the whole charged atmosphere of sixteenth century supper
strife. The currents of the age made a 'substantial agreement'
on the true meaning of sacrament and memorial impossible. [49]
Reacting against many undeniable abuses Cranmer said,

> 'The oblation and sacrifice of Christ in the mass is so called,
> not because Christ indeed is there offered and sacrificed by
> the priest and the people, (for that was done but once by
> himself upon the cross) but it is so called, because it is a
> memory and representation of that very true sacrifice and
> immolation which before was made upon the cross.'

Cranmer's fourth question was: 'Wherein consisteth the mass
by Christ's institution?' to which he replied by citing the central
eucharistic texts in the synoptics and Paul. 'The mass, by
Christ's institution, consisteth in those things which be set forth
in the evangelists, Mat. 26. Marc. 14. Luc. 22. 1 Cor. 10 and 11.'
The bishop of Durham called attention to Acts. The mass
consisted in thanksgiving and communion but also in the presentation of Christ and prayer for the whole church.

---

[49] Cf. Edward P. Echlin, *The Priest As Preacher, Past and Future*,
(Theology Today, no. 33), Cork, 1973, esp. pp. 79-87.

> 'The mass, by Christ's institution, consisteth in those things which be set forth by the evangelists, Matth. 26. Marc. 19. Luc. 22. and Paule, 1 Cor. 10.11. et 12. et Act 2. with humble and contrite confession, *the oblation of Christe,* as before: the receiving of the sacrament, giving of thanks therefore, and common prayer for the mystical body of Christe.'

Cranmer then asked 'What time the accustomed order began first in the church, that the priest alone should receive the sacrament?', and responded: 'I think the use, that the priest alone did receive the sacrament without the people, began not within six or seven hundred years after Christ.' Tunstall was more cautious about the date when the custom originated but blamed the tepidity and materialism of the laity for the abuse. 'The custom began, that the priest alone should receive the sacrament of necessity, when the people falling from devotion would not come to the communion, but cared more for their worldly business, than for godly receiving of the sacrament.'

Cranmer then asked the very pointed question, 'Whether it be convenient that the same custom continue still within this realm?' His own answer was: 'I think it more agreeable to the scripture and primitive church, that the first usage should be restored again, that the people should receive the sacrament with the priest.' Tunstall readily agreed that all present should communicate with the priest. However he was careful to add that if, through lack of devotion, the laity did not communicate, masses in which the priest alone received were legitimate.

> 'It were much convenient that people were exhorted to come to it oftener, if they could be brought thereto. Nevertheless if none will communicate, it is not meet that the priest stirred to communicate, should forbear for coldness or lack of other men's devotion.'

The seventh question dealt with stipendary masses for the dead, 'Whether it be convenient that masses satisfactory should continue, (that is to say) priests hired to sing for souls departed?' Cranmer replied in the negative. 'I think it not convenient that satisfactory masses should continue.' In effect the first non-papal archbishop of Canterbury was demanding a radical change in the contemporary mass system — the elimination from England of masses for the dead. Tunstall, defending the old order, oberved that in *every mass*, whether it was a stipendary mass or not, the priest was obliged to plead Christ's merits for the living and dead. As for stipendary masses, he justified the practice from Paul's letter to the Romans.

> 'All priests saying mass be bound in the same, to pray for the whole mystical body of Christe, quick and dead, though they be not hired thereto; and those that be deputed thereto, if they say mass, must do the same though they were not hired: and yet, as St Paule saith, Those that be partakers of spiritual things with other, ought to minister unto them temporal things in recompence, Rom. 15.'

Cranmer then asked if there should be a homily, 'Whether the gospel ought to be taught at the time of the mass, to the understanding of the people being present?' He replied that there should: 'I think it very convenient, that the gospel, concerning the death of Christ, and our redemption, should be taught to the people in the mass.' Tunstall agreed. But he observed that the homily was not the substance of the mass and that priests should preach outside of mass as well. 'It is much convenient that the gospel be taught to the understanding of the people being present, when it may be. Howbeit, it is not so of the substance of the mass, but the mass may be done without it, and it done at other times as well as at the mass.'

Cranmer asked when the practice of reservation began and, without supporting evidence, said, 'I think, six or seven hundred years after Christ.' Tunstall did not venture an answer, but the bishop of Lincoln thought it began with Innocent III. Dr Richard Cox 'supposed' the abuse crept in as early as the fifth century.

Finally Cranmer asked, 'When the hanging up of the same first began?' He thought it an invention 'of late times'. Cox was equally uncertain. 'When it began I cannot tell, and for what purpose it should hang there I cannot tell.'

From Cranmer's questions and his own confident answers we observe that he still retained the terms 'priest', 'altar', 'memorial', and 'representation'. But by 1548 the priest was, in

Cranmer's mature teaching, a minister of word and sacrament whose sacerdotal functions differed only in degree from those of the laity.

The Real Presence

We noticed that as early as 1538 Cranmer thought transubstantiation an 'opinion'.[50] In 1550 this 'opinion' was 'against all order and principles of nature and reason',[51] and innovation contrary to the evidence of the senses,[52] a false teaching contradictory to scripture, the early church, the eastern and western fathers, and historical theology.

> 'The testimony of the scripture, as by the consent of the old authors of Christ's church, both Greeks and Latins, from the beginning continually from time to time, that transubstantiation is against God's most holy word, against the old church of Christ, against all experience of our senses, against all reason, and against the doctrine of all ages, until the bishops of Rome devised the contrary.'[53]

Of paramount importance for an understanding of Cranmer's mature doctrine on the presence, the mass and the priesthood is his conviction that Christ's glorified body was circumscribed; Christ was 'in place' just as he had been before his ascension.[54] In other words *Christ* was in heaven, and not in the sacrament. Christ's presence in the recipient was similar to the sun's presence on earth. Both were really absent but their power effected persons on earth.

> 'As the sun corporally is ever in heaven, and no where else, and yet by his operation and virtue the sun is here in earth, by whose influence and virtue all things in the world be corporally regenerated, increased, and grow to their perfect state; so likewise our Saviour Christ bodily and corporally is in heaven, sitting at the right hand of

[50] 'Cranmer to Cromwell, 1538', in *Miscellaneous Writings*, p. 375.
[51] 'Answer to Gardiner' in *Writings and Disputations Relative to the Lord's Supper*, p. 250; cf. p. 253.
[52] Ibid., p. 255.
[53] Ibid., pp. 304-305; cf. pp. 301-302; 324-326.
[54] *Ibid.*, pp. 140-141; 375-376.

his Father, although spiritually he hath promised to be present with us upon earth unto the world's end.' [55]

If Christ was located in heaven and if a sacrament was a sign of something absent, then the eucharist was indeed a commemoration of a past act and the sacrament of an absent Christ. For Cranmer Christ's body 'was made' only once — and that was by the power of the Spirit in his birth from the Virgin Mary.

> 'They say, that the body of Christ is every day many times made, as often as there be masses said, and that then and there he is made of bread and wine. We say Christ's body was never but once made, and then not of the nature and substance of bread and wine, but of the substance of his blessed mother.' [56]

A real, 'gross' presence of Christ in the eucharist was a later invention of the Roman church; it was not the authentic teaching of Christ, the apostles or the evangelists. [57] This novel doctrine was introduced at the time of Berengarius. 'Sithens Christ's time the doctrine of my book was ever the catholic and public received faith of the church, until Nicholas the second's time, who compelled Berengarius to make such a devilish recantation, that the papists themselves be now ashamed of it.' [58]

Not that Cranmer denied an *effectual* presence of Christ in the eucharist. [59] 'The presence of Christ in his holy supper is a spiritual presence: and as he is spiritually present, so is he spiritually eaten of all faithful christian men, not only when they receive the sacrament, but continually so long as they be members spiritual of Christ's mystical body.' [60]

Bread and wine were 'figures' or 'sacraments' of Christ who was bodily, naturally, corporally, and really in heaven. When

---

[55] *Ibid.*, p. 89; cf. pp. 93-96; 100.
[56] *Ibid.*, p. 78; cf. pp. 249, 303.
[57] *Ibid.*, p. 283.
[58] *Ibid.*, p. 196; cf. p. 203.
[59] On this *all* Anglicans and Roman Catholics have always agreed. Cf. *Doctrine in the Church of England,* London, 1938, p. 165.
[60] 'Answer to Gardiner' in *Writings and Disputations Relative to the Lord's Supper,* p. 71.

F

presented by the priest they, through the *power* of Christ, spiritually nourished the recipient. In brief, figuratively Christ was in the elements, really he was in heaven, effectively he was within the recipient. "For figuratively he is in the bread and wine, and spiritually he is in them that worthily eat and drink the bread and wine; but really, carnally, and corporally, he is only in heaven, from whence he shall come to judge the quick and dead.' [61] For Cranmer the *unworthy* recipient encountered bread and wine; in Catholic teaching the sinner encountered Christ albeit not to the sinner's sanctification but to his perdition.

> 'No man can eat Christ's flesh and drink his blood but spiritually; which forasmuch as evil men do not, although they eat the sacramental bread until their bellies be full, and drink the wine until they be drunken, yet eat they neither Christ's flesh, nor drink his blood, neither in the sacrament nor without the sacrament, because they cannot be eaten and drunken but by spirit and faith.' [62]

Through a 'spiritual' eating the recipient enjoyed the grace and power of the redemption and deepened his integration into the mystical body. Cranmer realized whence his teaching diverged from Rome, having been a believer in Roman doctrine for most of his life. Even after his definitive break he desired unity in faith and what later ages would call intercommunion.

> 'God grant that, all contention set aside, both the parties may come to this holy communion with such a lively faith in Christ, and such an unfeigned love to all Christ's members, that as they carnally eat with their mouths this sacramental bread, and drink the wine, so spiritually they may eat and drink the very flesh and blood of Christ which is in heaven and sitteth on the right hand of his Father.' [63]

Cranmer compared the union of the communicant with Christ to the circuminsession of the Father and Son. 'For as his Father dwelleth in him, and he in his Father, and so hath life by his Father; so he that eateth Christ's flesh and drinketh his blood, dwelleth in Christ, and Christ in him, and by Christ he hath

---

[61] *Ibid.*, p. 139; cf. pp. 115-119; 140; 341-342; 371.

[62] *Ibid.*, p. 203; cf. pp. 214-219; 224; 341.

[63] *Ibid.*, p. 30; cf. pp. 46, 204, 219, 304, 328, 341-343.

eternal life.' [64] In fact Cranmer's teaching was substantially the same as that of Rome when he professed that the believing communicant was one with Christ for as long as he remained committed to the Lord in faith, hope and charity.

> 'They say, that Christ is really in the sacramental bread, being reserved a whole year, or so long as the form of bread remaineth: but after the receiving thereof he flieth up, say they, from the receiver unto heaven, as soon as the bread is chewed in the mouth, or changed in the stomach: but we say, that Christ remaineth in the man that worthily receiveth it, so long as the man remaineth a member of Christ.' [65]

Martin Bucer's influence appears in Cranmer's explanation that Christ is 'exhibited' to the receiver. When the priest presented the sacrament the faithful participated in the effects of the redemption. The sacrament was *unto the receiver* Christ's body and blood — but not through any *substantial* change wrought by the priest's words. Cranmer admitted *some* change in the consecrated elements just as he conceded *some* change in baptismal water blessed by a priest.

> 'For after consecration the body and blood of Christ be in them but as in figures, although in the godly receivers he is really present by his omnipotent power, which is as great as a miracle in our daily nourishing, as is wrought before in our regeneration. And therefore is Christ no less to be honoured of them that feed of him in his holy supper, than of them that he grafted in him by regeneration.' [66]

Yet this is 'receptionist' teaching. Although the elements *exhibited* Christ, he was present not in the sacrament but, through his power, in the recipient. 'In the Lord's supper, rightly used, is Christ's body exhibited indeed spiritually, and so really, if you take really to signify only a spiritual and not a corporal and carnal exhibition. But this real and spiritual exhibition is to the receivers of the sacrament, and not to the bread

---

[64] *Ibid.*, p. 207; cf. pp. 29, 43.

[65] *Ibid.*, p. 58; cf. p. 327.

[66] *Ibid.*, p. 282; cf. pp. 283, 328, 337.

and wine.' [67] 'I mean that he is present in the ministration and receiving of that holy supper according to his own institution and ordinance: like as in baptism, Christ and the Holy Ghost be not in the water, or font, but be given in the ministration, or to them that be truly baptized in the water.' [68]

Cranmer did not clearly perceive the significance of the traditional analogy between Jewish and Christian priesthood. Christian priesthood is analogous to existential *and* levitical priesthood. [69] For Cranmer the ordained priest ministered the elements within the baptismal priesthood. When the priest properly administered the sacrament Christ was present in the properly disposed recipients.

> 'They be no vain or bare tokens, as you would persuade, (for a bare token is that which betokeneth only and giveth nothing, as a painted fire, which giveth neither light nor heat;) but in the due ministration of the sacraments God is present, working with his word and sacraments. And although (to speak properly) in the bread and wine be nothing in deed to be worshipped, yet in them that duly receive the sacraments is Christ himself inhabiting, and is of all creatures to be worshipped.' [70]

In a rejoinder to the Catholic teaching of Richard Smith Cranmer shrewdly observed that his own doctrine differed from the Roman primarily in the 'how' of the presence. All Christians affirmed a reception of and incorporation into Christ. For the reformers Christ was not 'really' in the sacrament; for Roman Catholics Christ was really and mysteriously present in the eucharist as well as in the believing communicants.

> 'We receive the self-same body of Christ that was born of the virgin Mary, that was crucified and buried, that rose again, ascended into heaven, and sitteth at the right

---

[67] *Ibid.*, p. 123.

[68] *Ibid.*, p. 148; cf. pp. 158, 181, 227, 283.

[69] H. Elliott, 'The Elect and the Holy, an exegetical examination of 1 Peter 2.4-13 and the phrase *basilion hierateuma*', in *Supplements to Novum Testamentum,* Leiden, 1966, esp. pp. 185-188 and 200; cf. Robert F. Evans, *One and Holy, the Church in Latin Patristic Thought,* London, 1973, pp. 58-59.

[70] 'Answer to Gardiner' in *Writings and Disputations Relative to the Lord's Supper,* p. 11; cf. pp. 3, 340-341.

hand of God the Father Almighty: and the contention
is only in the manner and form how we receive it. . . . We
receive Christ spiritually by faith with our minds, eating
his flesh and drinking his blood: so that we receive Christ's
own very natural body, but not naturally nor corporally.
But this lying papist saith, that we eat his natural body
corporally with our mouths.' [71]

Cranmer's usual moderation was more manifest in his admission
that bread and wine *were consecrated* for a holy use. From this
it would have been a short step to *proclaim* a special presense of
Christ the high priest through the words and actions of his
ordained representative — and later Anglican authors were to
take this step. [72] Cranmer however did not take it. He did not
profess a new, unique, personal presence of *Christ* in the
eucharist itself. He was hampered by his theory of 'place'. Yet
he was intuitively aware that the priest had a special power to
repeat the dominical words as Christ's representative and that,
therefore, there was something special 'since apostolic times' in
the ordained Christian priesthood; and that, moreover, *something*
happened *even to the elements* when the priest repeated Christ's
words and deeds of the Last Supper. How close Cranmer came
to professing a special and personal presence of *Christ* in the
eucharist appears in the following quotation.

'When common bread and wine be taken and severed from
other bread and wine to the use of the holy communion,
that portion of bread and wine, although it be of the same
substance that the other is from the which it is severed,
yet it is now called consecrated, or holy bread and holy
wine. Not that the bread and wine have or can have any
holiness in them, but that they be used to an holy work,
and represent holy and godly things. . . . But specially they
may be called holy and consecrated, when they be separated
to that holy use by Christ's own words, which he spake
for that purpose, saying of the bread, "This is my body",
and of the wine, "This is my blood". [73]

---

[71] 'The Answer of Thomas, Archbishop of Canterbury 'etc' Against
the False Calumniation of Dr Richard Smith', *Ibid.*, p. 370.

[72] Edward P. Echlin, *The Anglican Eucharist in Ecumenical Perspective*, pp. 237-240.

[73] 'Answer to Gardiner', in *Writings and Disputations Relative to the
Lord's Supper*, p. 177; cf. pp. 180, 198, 182.

The Priest and Sacrifice

The one propitiatory sacrifice was that of Christ the high priest. In the Old Testament there had been figures of that forthcoming sacrifice; in the New there were commemorations of the saving event.

> 'The death of him upon the cross was the true sacrifice propitiatory, that purchased the remission of sin; which sacrifice continued not long, nor was made never but once. . . . Under pretence of holiness, the papistical priests have taken upon them to be Christ's successors, and to make such an oblation and sacrifice as never creature made but Christ alone, neither he made the same any more times than once, and that was by his death upon the cross.' [74]

In his Catholic days Cranmer had 'erred' in believing that priests offered propitiatory sacrifices.

> 'I confess of myself, that not long before I wrote the said catechism, I was in that error of the real presence, as I was many years past in divers other errors: as of transubstantiation, of the sacrifice propitiatory of the priests in the mass, of pilgrimages, purgatory, pardons, and many other superstitions and errors that came from Rome.' [75]

In his maturity Cranmer emphasized justification through faith in Christ's sacrifice. He acknowledged that justifying faith was related to good works. These 'works' however were in obedience to the divine commandments. The mass was not a divine commandment but an invention of the devil. It was simoniacal and blasphemous for the priest to offer propitiatory sacrifices.

> 'Three things, which must concur and go together in our justification: upon God's part, his great mercy and grace; upon Christ's part, justice, that is, the satisfaction of God's justice, or price of our redemption, by the offering of his body and shedding of his blood, with fulfilling of the law perfectly and thoroughly; and upon our part, true and

[74] *Ibid.*, p. 345.
[75] *Ibid.*, p. 374.

lively faith in the merits of Jesus Christ, which yet is not ours, but by God's working in us.' [76]

The mass was a human work, the worst of blasphemies because it implied there was something wanting in the propitiatory sacrifice of Christ.

'Let us rehearse some other kinds of papistical superstitions and abuses; as of beads, of lady psalters, and rosaries, of fifteen Oos, of St Barnard's verses, of St Agathe's letters, of purgatory, of masses satisfactory. . . . Such hath been the corrupt inclination of man, ever superstitiously given to make new honouring of God of his own head, and then to have more affection and devotion to observe that, than to search out God's holy commandments, and to keep them.' [77]

Therefore the daily offerings of priests for other persons, whether living or dead, were nugatory. A believer is saved through faith and receives communion for himself. Holy Communion is, moreover, a proclamation and testimony of salvation through faith.

'Godly people assembled together may receive the sacrament every man for himself, to declare that he remembereth what benefit he hath received by the death of Christ, and to testify that he is a member of Christ's body, fed with his flesh, and drinking his blood spiritually.' [78]

When Cranmer observed that the sole propitiatory sacrifice did not 'continue long' he was endorsing the destruction theory of sacrifice, an endorsement which, as we shall see, had fateful consequences for his conception of priesthood. 'The death of

---

[76] 'Homily of Salvation', in *Miscellaneous Writings*, p. 129; cf. 'Gardiner to Somerset, October 1547', in Foxe, *Acts and Monuments*, Vol. VI, pp. 45-50.

[77] 'Homily on Good Works', in *Miscellaneous Writings*, p. 148; cf. 'An Homily or Sermon of Good Works Annexed Unto Faith', in *English Reformers*, T.H.L. Parker, ed., London, 1966, pp. 283-286.

[78] *Archbishop Cranmer on the True and Catholic Doctrine and Use of the Sacrament of the Lord's Supper*, C.H.H. Wright, ed., London, 1907, p. 244; cf. Burnet, *The History of the Reformation*, Vol. V, p. 198 and John Strype, *Memorials of Archbishop Cranmer*, 3 Vols., Oxford, 1848, Vol. II, p. 43.

him upon the cross was the true sacrifice propitiatory, that
purchased the remission of sin; which sacrifice continued not
long, nor was made never but once.' [79] To call the Last Supper
a sacrifice would mean that Christ had offered many sacrifices
— every time he expressed his intention to die for sins.

> 'The scripture calleth not the declaration of Christ's will
> in his last supper to suffer death by the name of a sacrifice
> satisfactory for sin, nor saith not that he was there offered
> in deed. For the will of a thing is not in deed the thing.
> And if the declaration of his will to die had been an
> oblation and sacrifice propitiatory for sin, then had Christ
> been offered not only in his supper, but as often as he
> declared his will to die.' [80]

The sacrifice on the cross was all sufficient and needed no new
oblations of priests. 'Under pretence of holiness, the papistical
priests have taken upon them to be Christ's successors, and to
make such an oblation and sacrifice as never creature made but
Christ alone, neither he made the same any more times than
once, and that was by his death upon the cross.' [81] Transubstantiation and the oblations of priests were, thought Cranmer, the
matrix of the false Roman teaching on the mass, sacrifice and
priesthood. 'The roots of the weeds, is the popish doctrine of
transubstantiation, of the real presence of Christ's flesh and
blood in the sacrament of the altar (as they call it), and of the
sacrifice and oblation of Christ made by the priest, for the
salvation of the quick and the dead.' [82]

Nor was the mass the *same* sacrifice as Calvary. For, according to Cranmer, if the priest's sacrifice were identical with
Christ's it would still mean a daily slaying of Christ. Just as
Cranmer was hampered in his doctrine of the presence by his
philosophy of place — so in his doctrine of priesthood he was
hindered by his acceptance of a theory that every sacrifice meant
the slaying of a victim. Therefore the priest did not preside

[79] 'Answer to Gardiner', in *Writings and Disputations Relative to the
Lord's Supper,* p. 345; cf. p. 125.
[80] *Ibid.,* p. 86; cf. pp. 5, 345, 359.
[81] *Ibid.,* p. 345; cf. pp. 5, 47, 125, 348.
[82] 'A Preface to the Reader', *Ibid.,* p. 6.

at 'the selfsame sacrifice for sin that Christ himself made', for that would have been more wicked than the crime of 'the wicked Jews and Pharisees, which slew him and shed his blood but once.' [83]

The priest's oblation was not satisfactory. [84] At the eucharist *all* present offered themselves, their praise and thanksgiving, all proclaimed the good news of their justification through faith. Cranmer conceded, in this limited sense, that the mass *was* a sacrifice.

'I have denied that it is a sacrifice propitiatory for sin, or that the priest alone maketh any sacrifice there. For it is the sacrifice of all christian people to remember Christ's death, to laud and thank him for it, and to publish it and shew it abroad unto other, to his honour and glory.' [85]

To abort popular superstition about propitiatory masses and to mitigate strife among Englishmen the Edwardine Council in 1550 wrote to Bishop Ridley authorizing the removal of altars and the substitution of communion tables. Cranmer, as Archbishop of Canterbury, signed this significant document immediately after Protector Somerset.

'For the avoiding of all matters of further contention and strife about the standing or taking away of the said altars, to give substantial order throughout all your diocese, that with all diligence all the altars in every church or chapel, as well in places exempted, as not exempted, within your said diocese, be taken down, and in the stead of them a table to be set up in some convenient part of the chancel, within every such church or chapel, to serve for the ministration of the blessed communion.' [86]

---

[83] *Archbishop Cranmer on the True and Catholic Doctrine and Use of the Lord's Supper,* pp. 241-243; cf. 'Answer to Gardiner', in *Writings and Disputations Relative to the Lord's Supper,* p. 348.

[84] *Ibid.,* p. 81. 'Answer to Gardiner', in *Writings and Disputations Relative to the Lord's Supper.*

[85] 'The Answer of Thomas Archbishop of Canterbury etc. Against the False Calumniations of Dr Richard Smith', *Ibid.,* p. 369.

[86] 'The Council's Letter to Bishop Ridley to take down Altars, and place Communion Tables in their stead', in *Miscellaneous Writings,* p. 524; cf. Ridley, *Thomas Cranmer,* p. 312.

The first reason given for this radical innovation is noteworthy. An altar was conducive to the papist superstition of propitiatory masses and the daily immolation of Christ. A communion table signified that the Lord's Supper was a spiritual communion in Christ's body and blood.

> 'The form of a table shall more move the simple from the superstitious opinions of the Popish mass unto the right use of the Lord's Supper. For the use of an altar is to make sacrifice upon it: the use of a table is to serve for men to eat upon. Now when we come unto the Lord's board, what do we come for? To sacrifice Christ again, and to crucify him again; or to feed upon him that was once only crucified and offered up for us? If we come to feed upon him, spiritually to eat his body, and spiritually to drink his blood, which is the true use of the Lord's Supper; then no man can deny but the form of a table is more meet for the Lord's board than the form of an altar.' [87]

Cranmer thought his new Communion Service was in accord with scripture and the apostolic church. The mass was not.

> 'Thanks be to the eternal God! the manner of the holy communion, which is now set forth within this realm, is agreeable with the institution of Christ, with St Paul, and the old primitive and apostolic church, with the right faith of the sacrifice of Christ upon the cross for our redemption, and with the true doctrine of our salvation, justification, and remission of all our sins by that only sacrifice.' [88]

Cranmer did not waver from this conviction when, in 1553, the rumour circulated that he had restored the old order in his diocese. His outspoken and public denial of the rumour made his subsequent arrest inevitable.

> 'Now goeth the devil about by lying to overthrow the Lord's holy supper again, and to restore his Latin satisfactory mass, a thing of his own invention and device. And to bring the same the more easily to pass, some of his

---

[87] 'Reasons why the Lord's Board should be rather after the form of a Table than of an altar', in *Miscellaneous Writings*, pp. 524-525.

[88] 'Answer to Gardiner', in *Writings and Disputations Relative to the Lord's Supper*, p. 354; cf. E.P. Echlin, *The Anglican Eucharist in Ecumenical Perspective*, pp. 9-64.

inventors have abused the name of me, Thomas archbishop
of Canterbury, bruiting abroad that I have set up the mass
again in Canterbury ... the mass in many things not only
hath no foundation of Christ's apostles nor the primitive
church, but also is manifestly contrary to the same, and
containeth in it many horrible abuses.' [89]

Conclusion

Cranmer's doctrine on priesthood developed in a polemical
age which made serene discussions and — at least between
Roman Catholics and reformers — 'substantial agreements'
impossible. Even his mellifluous liturgies reflect the turbulent
context in which he laboured as scholar, courtier and admini-
strator.

Cranmer professed a special life-giving power of Christ
uniquely present in the eucharistic memorial. He taught that
the celebrant consecrated bread and wine to a holy use; even
after the Lord's Supper the remaining elements were to be
treated with reverence. He was reluctant, as we have seen, to
admit a personal presence of Christ in the memorial *itself*. His
position therefore was receptionist. Christ was personally present
in his power in the recipients. The elements while they were
consecrated and, to that extent, effective signs of Christ's power
were, nonetheless, signs of a (personally) absent Christ.

There was one Christian sacrifice, that of Christ on the
cross. The Last Supper was the institution of a memorial of that
one sacrifice. [90] Cranmer did not adequately distinguish the
existential priesthood of all God's people and the ordained
priesthood. [91] For Cranmer all Christians offered a spiritual

---

[89] 'A Declaration of Thomas Archbishop of Canterbury Concerning
the Untrue Report and Slander of Some, Which Reported, That
He Should Set Up Again the Mass in Canterbury', in *Writings and
Disputations Relative to the Lord's Supper*, p. 429.

[90] 'Answer to Gardiner', in *Writings and Disputations Relative to the
Lord's Supper*, p. 359.

[91] The Roman Catholic Sacred Congregation for the Doctrine of the
Faith seems aware of this important distinction in 'A Declaration

sacrifice of holy lives. In the cultic memorial of the one propitiatory sacrifice the priest's function differed from the laity's not
in essence but in degree. Still, there *was* a difference. The priest
prepared the Supper, read the gospel, preached the homily, and
presented the elements to the communicants. On the other hand
Cranmer emphasized that *all* participated in the cultic memorial
through the proclaimed 'Amen', all offered a sacrifice of praise,
remembrance, thanksgiving.

> 'Christ made no difference, but the difference that is
> between the priest and the layman in this matter is only
> in the ministration; that the priest, as a common minister
> of the church, doth minister and distribute the Lord's
> supper unto other, and other receive it at his hands. But
> the very supper itself was by Christ instituted and given
> to the whole church, not to be offered and eaten of the
> priest for other men, but by him to be delivered to all that
> would duly ask it.' [92]

Cranmer sometimes referred to a text in Peter Lombard that
had been a favourite with the great scholastics — the mass was
a representation and memorial of Christ's sacrifice. But for
Lombard and the scholastics the memorial was made with and
to God, pleading and enjoying the fruits of Christ's sacrifice.
For Cranmer the memorial was a manward remembrance and
proclamation. The difference between the two positions was
significant.

> 'How is it possible to set out more plainly the diversity
> of the true sacrifice of Christ made upon the altar of the
> cross, which was the propitiation of sin, from the sacrifice
> made in the sacrament, than Lombardus hath done in this
> place? For the one he calleth the true sacrifice, the other
> he calleth but a memorial or representation thereof, likening

for the Doctrine of the Faith, in defence of the Catholic Doctrine
on the Church against certain errors of the present Day', in *The
Tablet,* 14 July, 1973, pp. 667-670, esp. p. 669. R.H. Fuller does
not make the distinction in 'The Ministry in the New Testament',
in *Episcopalians and Roman Catholics, Can They Ever Get
Together,* Herbert J. Ryan and J. Robert Wright, eds., Danville,
1972, pp. 89-103.

[92] 'Answer to Gardiner', in *Writings and Disputations Relative to the
Lord's Supper,* p. 350; cf. pp. 346, 349, 352-353, 361-362.

the sacrifice made in the Lord's supper to a year's mind or
anniversary, whereat is made a memorial of the death of a
person, and yet it is not his death indeed. So in the Lord's
supper, according to his commandment, we remember his
death, preaching and commending the same until his return
again at the last day.' [93]

We repeat that for Cranmer there was something special about
the ordained ministry. While he reiterated the reformed shib-
boleth that the priest was minister of word and sacrament, the
priest's ministry of the word included the special power to
admit and exclude. In Cranmer's words,

'If they are much to be loved, honoured and esteemed,
that be the kings, chancellors, judges, officers, and ministers
in temporal matters: how much then are they to be
esteemed, that be ministers of Christ's words and sacraments, and have to them committed the keys of heaven,
to let in and shut out by the ministration of his word and
gospel?' [94]

And it was the *priest* who pronounced Christ's words of
institution. The *priest's* words consecrated material signs to a
holy use. [95] The *priest* distributed bread and wine which were
signs of Christ's effective presence in the recipients. [96] Cranmer
retained the nomenclature bishop, priest, deacon. All three
orders were related in a special way to the memorial of Christ's
sacrifice. What Jean Tillard says of the comprehensive Anglican
tradition of retaining a sacerdotal vocabulary is true not only of
late Anglicans, evangelical as well as Catholic, but of 'the
sensitive theilogian', Thomas Cranmer,

'Careful consideration of the major texts of the Anglican
tradition, incline one to think that the maintenance of
priestly vocabulary is not purely fortuitous; in spite of the
anti-sacrificial declaration which one constantly meets,
Anglicanism tries to remain loyal to the main thrust of
the common tradition of the church. Fidelity to the

[93] *Ibid.*, pp. 358-359.
[94] *Ibid.*, p. 350; cf. p. 363.
[95] *Ibid.*, p. 366.
[96] *Ibid.*

hierarchical structure "bishops, priests and deacons" reveals
an intuition that there is an interior quality of the apostolic
ministry, which the sacerdotal terms express, awkwardly
no doubt but still usefully.' [97]

[97] Jean Tillard, *What Priesthood Has the Ministry*, p. 7; cf. C.O.
Buchanan, E.L. Mascall, J.J. Packer, The Bishop of Willesden,
*Growing into Union, proposals for forming a United Church in
England*, London, 1970, pp. 69-84; and William Wand, 'Anglican
Eucharistic Theology in the Twentieth Century', *The Alcuin Club
Report*, 1972-1973, London, 1973, pp. 5-15, esp. pp. 13-15.

CHAPTER IV

The Edwardine Ordinals

'When the daye appoynted by the Bisshope is come, there shal be an exhortacio, declaring the duetie and office, of suche as come to be admitted Ministers, howe necessarie suche Orders are in the Churche of Christe, and also howe the people oughte to esteme them in theyr vocacion.'

The Edwardine Ordinal [1]

With the death of Henry VIII the English reformation notably quickened. Because of the pent up desire for liturgical change the first *Book of Common Prayer* went to the printers in 1549 without the inclusion of new ordination rites. But some extant original copies of the *Prayer Book* show that the Ordinal, itself in print by March, 1550, was meant to be included. [2]

Just as caution is desirable in assessing the Sarum rite so is it necessary in evaluating the two Ordinals put in use under

---

[1] First rubric for 'The Form and Manner of Ordering of Deacons' in *The First and Second Prayer Books of Edward VI*, W. Benham, ed., London, n.d., p. 273. All references to Cranmer's Ordinals will be taken from Benham's verbatim reprint of one of the four original editions printed by Grafton and now housed in the British Museum. Subsequent quotations will be modernized for the convenience of the reader save only where modernization might distort the original meaning.

[2] *Ibid.*, p. 270, note.

Edward VI. [3] In the Ordinals Archbishop Cranmer omitted explicit references to sacrifice and medieval additions to the pontifical which were believed to signify the power of sacrifice. In studying Cranmer's Ordinals it is necessary to call attention to his *omissions* of sacrificial symbolism just as in assessing Sarum it is necessary to attend to later *additions* to the rite which positively signified the priest's power at the eucharist. Caution is necessary because in many respects Cranmer's Ordinals were comprehensive rites. Cranmer included and in many ways improved upon many features of the pontifical. Therefore to give a reasonably balanced picture of what Cranmer accomplished we shall attend to what he *did* as well as to what he omitted. [4]

The place to begin an assessment of Cranmer's Ordinal is with the title and preface to the reformed rite. The Edwardine Ordinal was entitled, 'The form and manner of making and consecrating of Archbishops, Bishops, Priests and Deacons.' This title is important. Minor orders were excluded — but the Ordinal was intended to continue the ministry which had developed in the primitive church. Cranmer drafted a rite to convey the ministry which is reflected in the writings and redactions in the New Testament and in the earliest Christian authors. [5] The reformed church order 'as accepted in England' took account of development, albeit not sacrificial development, which took place under the Spirit's guidance in the first decades of the life of the Christian community. The title itself indicates that there was to be no radical retrenchment to a 'canon within the canon' nor to a 'pre-Catholic' church order. There was to be no purely presbyteral ordering and certainly no purely

---

[3] Cf. *supra,* pp. 4-5.

[4] This method has not always been followed and the result is unfair to Cranmer's rite. Cf. for example Messenger, *The Reformation, the Mass, and Priesthood, passim,* and Clark, *Eucharistic Sacrifice and the Reformation,* pp. 191-194.

[5] For a brief study of the distinction between Christ's teaching and apostolic and sub-apostolic writings pertaining to the ministry cf. R.H. Fuller, 'The Ministry in the New Testament', in *Episcopalians and Roman Catholics, Will They Ever Get Together?,* pp. 88-103; cf. also R.E. Brown, *Priest and Bishop,* N.Y. 1970, chapter 2.

charismatic ordering. For the English reformers the distinction
was not between hierarchical and charismatic order but between
authentic order according to scripture and the early Christian
writings and inauthentic order rooted in the 'popish weeds' of
transubstantiation and the priest's power to offer for the quick
and the dead. [6] While Cranmer intended to uproot the latter
ordering in the English lands he was resolved to maintain the
development of priestly terminology and a triadic ministry. All
of this is attested at least implicitly in the title of the new
Ordinal.

And it is further explained in Cranmer's very important and
very nuanced Preface. [7] Cranmer, three centuries before the
advanced scholarship of twentieth century exegesis and the
reflection of that scholarship in the event of Vatican II, used
language remarkably similar to that Council when he began his
Preface, 'It is evident unto all men, diligently readinge holye
scripture, and auncient aucthours, that fro the Apostles tyme,
there hathe bene these orders of Ministers in Christes church,
Bisshoppes, Priestes, and Deacons'. [8] Four points are especially
noteworthy. Firstly, Cranmer endorses primitive development
in Christian ministry when he cites 'ancient authors' as witnesses
along with scripture. Secondly, Cranmer does not say that
Christ 'instituted' the triadic ministry nor that the apostles were
the first bishops. He *does* say that these orders had existed from
the time of the apostles, thereby attributing great importance

---

[6] Thomas Cranmer, 'A Preface to the Reader', in *Writings and
Disputations Relative to the Lord's Supper,* p. 6.
[7] The preface is significant and important because it gives a succinct
statement of Cranmer's intention in framing the Ordinal in 1550.
It is also important because of the attention intermittently focused
upon it since its presentation to the commission in January 1550.
Cf. for example J.J. Hughes' use of the preface in his defence of
Anglican Orders in *Stewards of the Lord,* pp. 227-228; and Francis
Clark's defence of *Apostolicae Curae* in *Anglican Orders and Defect
of Intention,* pp. 174-179.
[8] Vatican II used remarkably similar but more nuanced language when,
speaking of the triadic ministry, it said, 'Thus, the divinely established ecclesiastical ministry is exercised on different levels by those
who from antiquity have been called bishops, priests and deacons',
in The Dogmatic Constitution on the Church, 3, 28, in *The
Documents of Vatican II,* Walter Abbott ed., N.Y., 1966, p. 53.

G

to the Pastoral epistles and the later Lucan and Johannine
writings. Thirdly, Cranmer continues the tradition embedded
in the Verona Sacramentary when he refers to Bishops, Priests
and Deacons as 'orders' in the church. Finally, while sacerdotal
terminology is retained Cranmer clearly identifies the hierarchy
as 'ministers'.

The preface continues,

> 'which Offices were evermore had in such reverent estima-
> tion, that no man by his own private authority, might
> presume to execute any of them, except he were first
> called, tried, examined, and known, to have such qualities,
> as were requisite for the same. And also by public prayer,
> with imposition of hands, approved, and admitted there-
> unto.'

In other words these 'offices' are of such vital importance for
the life and continuance of the community that no man may
presume to exercise them on his own authority. In addition to
his response to an interior call or 'vocation' he must also be
called, tried and approved by the community. Nor is mere
appointment by the godly prince or acceptance by the community of those who come forward as ministers adequate. Those
who are elected must be admitted to their respective orders in a
public ceremony through prayer and imposition of hands.
Therefore Cranmer did not consider the Church in England to
be in an emergency situation similar to that which he had
described in 1540. [9] It was just such an emergency situation
that the Ordinal was intended to avoid by providing the Church
of England with a form and manner of ordering which would
preserve the continuation, what later ages would call the
apostolic succession, in the ministry.

For the Preface proceeds,

> 'And therefore to the intent these orders should be con-
> tinued, and reverently used, and esteemed in this Church
> of England, it is requisite that no man (not being at this
> present Bishop, Priest, nor Deacon) shall execute any of

---

[9] Cf. 'Questions and Answers Concerning the Sacraments', in
Miscellaneous Writings, p. 11.

them, except he be called, tried, examined, and admitted, according to the form hereafter following.'

The intention of the authors of the Ordinal — and this has importance for the 'form' of the rite in the later Roman-canonical sense — was that the apostolic ministry should be continued in the Church of England according to the form and manner of the Ordinal.

The central importance of *episcopal* ordering is clearly stated in the conclusion to the Preface.

'And the Bishop knowing, either by himself, or by sufficient testimony, any person to be a man of virtuous conversation, and without crime, and after examination and trial, finding him learned in the Latin tongue, and sufficiently instructed in holy Scripture, may upon a Sunday or Holy-day, in the face of the church, admit him a deacon or priest or bishop in such manner and form, as hereafter followeth.'

The bishop is responsible for the examination, admission and ordination of worthy candidates. He is to have moral certitude that deacons, who in the sixteenth century concept of an ascending hierarchy were to aspire to 'higher' orders, were virtuous and sufficiently learned for admission to their order. If the candidate had these qualities the bishop was to admit him publicly 'in the face of the church.'

The Preface to the Ordinal clearly teaches the antiquity and apostolicity of the threefold hierarchy; it clearly teaches that public ordering through prayer and imposition of hands is the accepted way to continue this ministry; it clearly teaches the intention of the authors of the Ordinal to continue this ministry in England; it clearly teaches that the bishop is responsible for the admission and ordination of ministers and that he is to ordain them publicly according to the form of the Ordinal. There is no warrant to doubt that the authors of the Ordinal intended to continue the ministry as it had been exercised since apostolic times.

There is, however, some room for debate about the authors' *understanding* of that ministry and therefore about the comprehensiveness of the Ordinal's signification. We have observed

where Cranmer's understanding of the ministry diverged from
the teaching of Stephen Gardiner and the Sarum rite. His
Ordinal reflects — and was meant to reflect — his teaching and
that divergence. The question confronting a later age within
a different historical context is whether or not the rite adequately
includes and signifies the eucharistic office of the ministry and,
if it does not, whether or not other churches sharing the common
heritage can acknowledge Anglican ministry as complete. Before
Anglicans and Roman Catholics, whose leaders have expressed
agreement on the meaning and purpose of ministry, can resolve
these problems it is desirable to have some familiarity not only
with Cranmer's teaching and the contemporary Roman teaching
from which he diverged but also to have reasonable familiarity
with Cranmer's two Ordinals which have left their traces in all
subsequent Anglican Ordinals and ordinations. [10]

THE ORDINAL OF 1550

The Ordering of Deacons

The rite for diaconal ordination concerns us because deacons
are within the hierarchical ministry and because the form for
their ordination illuminates the doctrine and rites of priesthood
and episcopacy. The rite for the ordination of deacons opened
with a rubric virtually identical with the inauguration rubric for
the ordering of priests. It stated that on ordination day there
was to be an exhortation concerning 'the duty and office, of
such as come to be admitted Ministers, how necessary such
Orders are in the Church of Christ, and also how the people
ought to esteem them in their vocation.' Each order or office
enjoys its distinctive responsibilities and functions; the officers
are called ministers, servants not lords of God's people; the
offices of deacon, priest and bishop are necessary in the church
and to be esteemed by the faithful.

After the presentation of candidates the bishop repeated what
was to be reiterated throughout the Ordinal — that ministers

---

[10] H.F. Woodhouse, *The Doctrine of the Church in Anglican Theology,
1547-1603*, London, 1954, pp. 95-106.

must be both virtuous and learned. This emphasis was in harmony with all the early ordination rites extending back to the Apostolic Tradition of Hippolytus (c. 215) which itself reflected doctrine and practice in second century Rome.[11] We noticed that holiness was emphasized more than cult in the Sarum pontifical. Cranmer retained this healthy emphasis and in his insistence on learning — for the minister's service of the word — improved upon Sarum. 'Take heed that the persons whom ye present unto us, be apt and meet, for their learning and godly conversation, to exercise their ministry duely, to the honour of God, and edifying of his Church.'

Before the rite for deacons began the congregation was invited to reveal any notable defect in the candidates which rendered them unworthy of ordination. If any diriment crime was alleged the accused was not ordained unless and until he was able to 'try himself clear of that crime'.

In the revised litany within the ordination ceremony a petition was inserted concerning the 'bishop' of Rome which at least obliquely referred to the ministry when it asked deliverance from false doctrine, heresy and contempt of God's word and commandments.

'From all sedition and secret conspiracy, from the tyranny of the Bishop of Rome, and all his detestable enormities, from all false doctrine and heresy, from hardness of heart, and contempt of thy word and commandment.
Good lord, deliver us.'

In a collect following the litany there was a pointed reference to 'our only mediator and advocate Jesus Christ'. There was also the refrain that ordinands should be replenished 'with the truth of thy doctrine, and innocence of life, that, both by word and good example, they may faithfully serve thee in this office'. Preaching, as was also emphasized in Sarum and the early ordination rites, was through word and example.

On days when only deacons were ordained the epistle was taken from the passage referring to deacons in 1 Timothy, a

---

[11] Edward P. Echlin, *The Priest as Preacher*, pp. 34-36.

selection which again alluded to holiness in the minister — and
in his wife. On days when priests were ordained the preceeding
passage in the epistle relating to *episcopoi* was also read.

Between epistle and gospel deacons and 'every of them that
are to be ordained' took the oath of royal supremacy 'against
the usurped power and authority of the Bishop of Rome'.

Within the rite for ordination of deacons there was an
examination of candidates which explained the deacons' relationship to priests with whom they served. Deacons assisted at
worship especially when the priest 'ministreth Holy Communion'. They were permitted to preach in the Christian assembly
if they were licensed by the diocesan bishop. Their ministry
of charity took the form of intermediation, the deacon informing
the curate of the needs of God's people. This examination —
which comprehends the deacon's traditional ministry of liturgy,
word and charity — makes no mention of the eucharist in
sacrificial terminology.

> 'It pertains to the office of a Deacon in the Church where
> he shall be appointed to assist the Priest in divine service,
> and especially when he ministers the holy Communion,
> and to help him in distribution thereof, and to read holy
> scriptures and Homilies in the congregation, and to
> instruct the youth in the Catechism, to Baptize and to
> preach if he be admitted thereto by the Bishop. And
> furthermore, it is his office where provision is so made to
> search for the sick, poor, and impotent people of the parish,
> and to intimate their estates, names, and places where they
> dwell to the Curate, that by his exhortation they may be
> relieved by the parish or other convenient alms: will you
> do this gladly and willingly?'

A carefully phrased question about leaders in the church
indicates that according to the Ordinal bishops enjoyed a special
power of leadership.

> 'Will you reverently obey your ordinary and other chief
> Ministers of the Church, and them to whom the government
> and charge is committed over you, following with a glad
> mind and will their godly admonitions?'

Ordination through prayer and imposition of hands followed the
Communion Service. The newly ordained deacons were then

given the bible, symbolizing their ministry of the word. A final collect refers to the diaconate as an inferior grade from which deacons were to ascend to 'higher ministries'.

> 'Make them we beseech thee, O Lord, to be modest, humble, and constant in their ministration, to have a ready will to observe all spiritual discipline, that they having always the testimony of a good conscience, and continuing ever stable and strong in thy son Christ, may so well use themselves in this inferior office, that they may be found worthy to be called unto the higher ministers in thy Church.'

The one final rubric stipulated that deacons were to remain in their order for a year unless their Ordinary provided otherwise. If the deacon remained faithful and diligent in his ministry he was to be admitted to the office of priesthood.

> 'He must continue in that office of a Deacon, the space of a whole year at the least (except for reasonable causes, it be otherwise seen to his ordinary) to the intent he may be perfect, and well expert in the things appertaining to the Ecclesiastical administration, in executing whereof, if he be found faithful and diligent, he may be admitted by his Diocesan to the order of Priesthood.'

Cranmer's revised ordination rite for deacons is inextricably connected with his doctrine of priesthood and episcopacy. The diaconate was an order, the lowest in the hierarchy, which had existed since apostolic times. In ordinary circumstances the deacon was expected to ascend to the priesthood. Cranmer retained the imposition of hands with prayer and he used sacerdotal terms. The triadic hierarchy was portrayed as no arbitrary ordering but as necessary for the church. The holiness and learning of ordained ministers — preaching in both the wide and strict sense — was emphasized throughout. According to the prayers and rubrics in the ordination rite for deacons the priest enjoyed special powers of preaching and of administering Communion; the bishop was endowed with special powers of leadership; the deacon was subordinate and ancillary to these higher offices. Nowhere in the rite for diaconal ordination is there reference to any power of sacrifice endemic in the priesthood. In fact the rite pointedly recalls the unique mediation of

Christ and the priest's role at the 'Holy Communion' as one of ministering.

Cranmer's omission of sacrificial symbolism (while retaining, however, the priestly title) was no oversight. These omissions are more obvious and of fateful importance in the ordination rite for priests.

The Ordering of Priests

The 1550 'Form of ordering Priests' began with a psalm, which could be read or sung, and two selections from the New Testament: Paul's address to the elders of Ephesus (Acts 20, 17-38) and his instructions to Timothy about the appointment and qualification of *episcopoi* and deacons (1 Tim 3, 1-7). These selections clearly imply that priests succeed the apostles, their delegates, and the residential guardian-presbyters. They emphasize the requisite virtue in priests and their ministry of preaching, leadership and service. Neither selection, nor that for the gospel, contains any explicit mention of the priest's power at the eucharist.

The gospel selections were the commission of the apostles in Matt. (28, 20), the parable of the Good Shepherd in John (10, 1-16), and the commission of the apostles in John (20, 19-23). All these selections emphasize the ministry of teaching, leadership and sanctifying.

Following the gospel and a hymn to the Holy Spirit the bishop presented the ordinands to the congregation as those 'whom we purpose God willing, to receive this day, unto the holy office of Priesthood'. As in the rite for deacons the people were invited to voice objections to the candidates' worthiness for the office. If no objections were forthcoming the rite continued with a litany containing a collect which referred to the divine establishment of diverse orders in the church. Priests, excelling in doctrine and virtue, were called to give glory to God and service to the church. There was no explicit mention of a role at the eucharist.

> 'Almighty God, giver of all good things, which thy holy
> spirit has appointed diverse orders of Ministers in thy

church, mercifully behold these thy servants, now called to the Office of Priesthood, and replenish them so with the truth of thy doctrine, and innocence of life, that both by word and good example, they may faithfully serve thee in this office, to the glory of thy name, and profit of the congregation, through the merits of our saviour Jesus Christ.'

After the oath of supremacy and repudiation of Rome there followed an address to the ordinands. The office of priesthood was called an office of singular importance and dignity, for priests were 'the messengers, the watchmen, the Pastors, and the stewards of the Lord'. They were to teach, admonish and provide for the Lord's family, his flock and his children. Priests proclaimed the word and instructed the faithful. They served the church and congregation which is the Body of Christ, unifying his people in faith and holiness.

'Consider with yourselves the end of your ministry, towards the children of God, towards the spouse and body of Christ, and see that you never cease your labour, your care and diligence, until you have done all that lies in you, according to your bounden duty, to bring all such as are, or shall be committed to your charge, unto that agreement in faith, and knowledge of God, and to that ripeness, and perfectness of age in Christ, that there be no place left among them, either for error in Religion, or for viciousness in life.'

Only with the grace of the Holy Spirit can the ordinand fulfil his calling. Nor can the same Holy Spirit use the priest as an instrument of salvation unless his doctrine and life are in conformity with scripture. Therefore the priest must dedicate himself to a lifelong study of theology and model his own life and those committed to his pastoral care on the teaching of the bible. So exigitive is a life dedicated to ministry of the gospel that the priest must put behind him profane pursuits.

'Forasmuch as your office is both of so great excellency, and of so great difficulty, you see with how great care and study you ought to apply yourselves, as well that you may show yourselves kind to that Lord, who has placed you in so high a dignity, as also to beware, that neither you yourselves offend, neither be occasion that other offend.

Howbeit, you cannot have a mind and a will thereto of yourselves, for that power and ability is given of God alone. Therefore you see how you ought and have need, earnestly to pray for his holy spirit. And seeing that you cannot by any other means compass the doing of so weighty a work pertaining to the salvation of man, but with doctrine and exhortation, taken out of holy scripture and with a life agreeable unto the same. You perceive how studious you ought to be in reading and learning the holy scriptures, and in framing the manners, both of yourselves, and of them that specially pertain unto you, according to the rule of the same scriptures. And for this selfsame cause, you see how you ought to forsake and set aside (as much as you may) all worldly cares and studies.'

The priest's prayer for the assistance of the Holy Spirit was 'by the mediation of our only mediator and saviour Jesus Christ'. Cranmer repeated what subsequent history has shown can never be repeated too often: the priest must *daily* study and contemplate scripture, sanctify himself and his people according to scripture, and be an example of Christian life to his flock.

'We have a good hope, that you have well weighed and pondered these things with yourselves, long before this time, and that you have clearly determined, by God's grace, to give yourselves wholly to this vocation, whereunto it hath pleased God to call you, so that (as much as lies in you) you apply yourselves wholly to this one thing, and draw all your cares and studies this way, and to this end. And that you will continually pray for the heavenly assistance of the holy ghost, from God the father, by the mediation of our only mediator and saviour Jesus Christ, that by daily reading and weighing of the scriptures, you may so endeavour yourselves from time to time sanctify the lives of you and yours, and to fashion them after the rule and doctrine of Christ. And that you may be wholesome and godly examples and patterns for the rest of the congregation to follow.'

The public examination of candidates that followed the admonition was an aid to the ordinand himself and a witness to the congregation of his intention to fulfil his responsibilities.

'That this present congregation of Christ here assembled, may also understand your minds and wills, in these things:

> And that this your promise, shall more move you to do your duties, you shall answer plainly to these things, which we in the name of the congregation shall demand of you, touching the same.'

Neither in the admonition nor in the examination was there reference to consecration, sacrifice or mediation. By omitting such references Cranmer signified a less comprehensive priesthood than did the Sarum pontifical. In the admonition and examination Sarum no less than the Ordinal had emphasized holiness and learning. But Sarum had referred to the priest's role as mediator, 'As good mediators between God and men they convey the precepts of God to the people by preaching the truth, and they offer the prayers of the people to God by interceding for sinners'; and Sarum, referring to the Last Supper, had attended explicitly to the priest's role at the altar. 'How great is the excellence of the sacerdotal office, through which daily on the altar the passion of Christ is celebrated and the sinner, converted from his sins, is reconciled to God.'

In the examination of candidates the Ordinal testified to the distinctive patrimony of the English church when the candidate was asked if he believed himself called to the priesthood according to the will of Christ *and* 'the order of this Church of England'.

> 'Do you think in your heart, that you be truly called according to the will of our Lord Jesus Christ, and the order of this Church of England, to the ministry of Priesthood?
>
> *Answer*: I think it.'

The candidate was then asked to profess his belief that scripture contained all that is necessary for salvation through faith in Jesus Christ. He was to teach nothing as necessary for salvation which could not be proved in scripture. The intent of this part of the examination was surely polemical; and the historical context indicates that one alleged accretion Cranmer was attacking was the sacrificial dimension in Christian priesthood.

> 'Be you persuaded that the holy Scriptures contain sufficiently all doctrine required of necessity for eternal salvation, through faith in Jesus Christ? And are you determined

with the said scriptures, to instruct the people committed
to your charge, and to teach nothing, as required of
necessity, to eternal salvation, but that you shall be
persuaded may be concluded, and proved by the scripture?

Answer: I am so persuaded, and have so determined by
God's grace.'

The priest was a minister of the word, sacraments and discipline
as the Lord had commanded 'and as this realm has received the
same'.

'Will you then give your faithful diligence always, so to
minister the doctrine and Sacraments, and the discipline
of Christ, as the Lord hath commanded, and as this realm
hath received, the same, according to the commandments
of God, so that you may teach the people committed to
your cure and charge, with all diligence to keep and observe
the same?

Answer: I will so do, by the help of the Lord.'

The priest was to guard against false doctrine and when
necessary to admonish his flock.

'Will you be ready with all faithful diligence, to banish and
drive away all erroneous and strange doctrines, contrary to
God's word, and to use both public and private admonitions
and exhortations, as well to the sick as to the whole, within
your cures, as need shall require and occasion be given?

Answer: I will, the Lord being my helper.'

The examination repeated what the admonition had taught about
a priest's scholarship, that the priest as a man of prayer and
diligent student of scripture and those branches of learning
ancillary to scripture was to forsake merely profane learning.

'Will you be diligent in prayers, and in reading of the holy
scriptures, and in such studies as help to the knowledge
of the same, laying aside the study of the world and the
flesh?

Answer: I will endeavour myself so to do, the Lord being
my helper.'

Ordinal priests were to be free to marry. Those who did marry
would be assisted in their ministry by families who would

fashion their lives according to scripture and thereby be examples to the entire congregation.

> 'Will you be diligent to frame and fashion your own selves, and your families, according to the doctrine of Christ, and to make both yourselves and them (as much as in you lies) wholesome examples and spectacles to the flock of Christ?
>
> *Answer*: I will so apply myself, the Lord being my helper.'

The priest was a minister of peace and love especially among those committed to his care.

> 'Will you maintain and set forward (as much as lies in you) quietness, peace and love amongst all christian people, and especially them that are, or shall be committed to your charge?
>
> *Answer*: I will so do, the Lord being my helper.'

The priest of the second rank was to obey his bishop 'and other chief ministers'.

> 'Will you reverently obey your Ordinary, and other chief ministers, unto whom the government and charge is committed over you, following with a glad mind and will, their godly admonition, and submitting yourselves to their godly judgements?
>
> *Answer*: I will so do, the Lord being my helper.'

The public examination of priests — itself a form of preaching — concluded with a prayer by the presiding bishop petitioning God who had given the intention to proceed to the priesthood that he would also provide the grace of fruition.

> 'Almighty God, who hath given you this will to do all these things, grant also unto you strength and power to perform the same, that he may accomplish his work which he has begun in you, until the time he shall come at the latter day, to judge the quick and the dead.'

Thus, in the introductory ceremonies of the Ordinal all mention of priestly mediation, consecration and sacrifice — which were included in the introductory parts of the Sarum ordination rite — were deleted. The rite thus far, as we have already observed, was comprehensive except for this deliberate and weighty

omission. The same may be said for what follows — the preface
to the ordination prayer, the tradition of instruments, the
Communion Service, and the concluding prayer and rubrics.

The preface recalls the perfection of redemption wrought
through Jesus Christ. There is an interesting inclusion referring
to church order at Ephesus. Christ sent not only apostles but
(according to the epistle to the Ephesians) prophets, evangelists,
leaders and pastors. Priests therefore are successors not only
of the apostles, apostolic delegates and residential presbyters,
but also of prophets, evangelists and pastor-teachers. This
allusion to New Testament church order demonstrates Cranmer's
keen familiarity with the New Testament and his oft-repeated
emphasis on the primacy of preaching. Also important is his
emphasis on the episcopal and priestly task of glorifying God
and extending the kingdom. These inclusions in the preparatory
prayer to ordination place the priest within the community as
a leader of God's people and minister of the word in service of
the kingdom of God. However, within the context of the
Edwardine reformation Cranmer's *total* omission of cultic references was an over-reaction. We repeat that he was breaking
not only with the many abuses and superstitions of his time —
which break was itself commendable — but with the doctrine
of priesthood which had developed in the early church. His
preface — and the entire Ordinal — was defective in its significant non-signification of the priest's power at the eucharistic
memorial. His beautiful preparatory prayer began as follows,

> 'Almighty God and heavenly father, which of thy infinite
> love and goodness towards us, hast given to us thy only
> and most dear beloved son Jesus Christ.'

Then the bishops and priests present imposed hands on the
ordinand(s) with a prayer which was significant *in what it
omitted,* not because the prayer in itself was incapable of serving
as an 'irreducible minimum' to confer Christian priesthood but
because of the entire context of the Ordinal and its composition.

> 'Receive the holy ghost, whose sins you do forgive, they
> are forgiven: and whose sins you do retain, they are
> retained: and be you a faithful dispenser of the word of
> God, and of his holy Sacraments. In the name of the father,
> and of the son, and of the holy ghost. Amen.'

Thereafter Cranmer retained one late medieval addition to the ancient ordination rites — the tradition of instruments, namely the chalice and eucharistic bread. Yet in the Ordinal this rite was intended to signify and convey what the rest of the rite signified and conveyed — the priest was a minister of the word (the bible) and sacraments (the chalice and bread). Before recording Cranmer's accompanying prayer it is most instructive to recall the Sarum prayer at this moment in the ceremony. 'Receive the power to offer sacrifice to God, and to celebrate Mass, both for the living and the dead.' The Sarum signification therefore was clear and unequivocal; for a rite derives its signification mainly from the words spoken. Cranmer's prayer gave the rite quite another signification. The contrast between the two prayers or 'forms' vividly demonstrates where Cranmer diverged from traditional teaching on priesthood and where his rite's signification differed from that of the pontifical. Realizing that *lex orandi est lex credendi* Cranmer endeavoured to teach and signify a reformed concept of priesthood. Therefore the instruments were accompanied by these words, 'Take your authority to preach the word of God, and to minister the holy Sacraments in this congregation, where you shall be so appointed.'

We repeat that priests *are* primarily ministers of the word and sacraments. But an apostolic ministry as reflected 'in holy scripture and the ancient authors' comprehends a dimension which Cranmer omitted from his Ordinal. In other circumstances than those of sixteenth century England the omission of references to the power of sacrifice would not necessarily have vitiated the signification of the rite. But 'the native character and spirit' of the Ordinal and its historical background made these omissions momentous. The conclusion to the ordination rite for priests is consistent with the entire context of the Ordinal.

> 'Most merciful father, we beseech you so to send upon these your servants your heavenly blessing, that they may be clad about with all justice, and that your word spoken by their mouths may have such success, that it may never be spoken in vain. Grant also that we may have grace to hear, and receive the same as your most holy word and the means of our salvation, that in all our words and

deeds we may seek your glory, and the increase of your
kingdom, through Jesus Christ our Lord. Amen.'

In a word, Cranmer's omissions are as significant as what he
included in his rite. There are no references to the altar, no
analogies with the sons of Aaron, no comparison of priests to
levites, no unction or references to the priest's hands, no tradition of stole and chasuble. In the Sarum rite whenever the
priest's sacramental functions were enumerated his role at the
altar was included; in Cranmer's Ordinal it was studiously
omitted. The priest was portrayed as a successor to the ministry
of apostles, prophets, evangelists, pastors and teachers which for
Cranmer, no less than for the later precisionists or Puritans,
precluded sacrifice because this was not believed to be explicitly
commanded in scripture. In an important medieval addition
which Cranmer retained, the tradition of instruments, the
accompanying prayer altered the traditional meaning.

The Consecration of Bishops

'The Form of Consecrating of an Archbishop or Bishop'
is remarkably similar to the form and manner of ordaining
priests. The introit and epistle are the same. We have noticed
that Cranmer was sympathetic with the theory extending back
to Jerome and Ambrosiaster of a 'parity' of ministers. [12] The
epistle and the thrust of the following prayers and ceremonies
favour this theory. The bishop is portrayed as one who differs
from the priest in his *authority* and in his power to confirm and
ordain, powers which were given to him by the church. There
is no signification of the fullness of priesthood in Cranmer's
consecration rite.

After the gospel which was 'as before in the ordering of
priests' two bishops, vested in surplice and cope and with pastoral
staffs, presented the elect, also vested in surplice and cope, to
the presiding archbishop with the words, 'Most reverend father

---

[12] 'Questions and Answers Concerning the Sacraments', in *Miscellaneous Writings,* p. 117.

in God, we present unto you this godly and well learned man to be consecrated Bishop.' The archbishop or an assistant read the royal mandate for the consecration and the oath 'touching the acknowledgement of the king's supremacy, shall be administered to the person elected, as it is set out in the Order of Deacons.' This was followed by an oath of obedience to the archbishop.

'In the name of God, Amen. I, N. chosen Bishop of the Church of N. do profess and promise, all due reverence and obedience to the Archbishop, and to the Metropolitan church of N. and to their successors: so help me God, and his holy gospel.'

The bidding prayer served to remind the congregation that vocation to the episcopate was a call of the Holy Spirit, that a candidate was to be admitted publicly by an archbishop according to the form of the Ordinal and that bishops were successors of the twelve and the other apostles. The prayer was a public endorsement by the Church of England of the authenticity of the development of a mono-episcopate and the institutionalization of the gifts of leadership in the church.

'Brethren, it is written in the gospel of saint Luke, that our saviour Christ continued the whole night in prayer, before ever that he did choose and send forth his twelve Apostles. It is written also in the Acts of the Apostles, that the disciples which were at Antioch did fast and pray, before ever they laid hands upon, or sent forth Paul and Barnabas. Let us therefore, following the example of our saviour Christ and his Apostles, first fall to prayer, or that we admit and send forth this person presented unto us, to the work whereunto we trust the holy ghost has called him.'

The litany included the following prayer which signified the bishop's service of God and the church.

'That it may please you to bless this our brother elected, and to send your grace upon him, that he may duly execute the office whereunto he is called, to the edifying of your Church, and to the honour, praise and glory of your name.

Answer: We beseech you to hear us good Lord.'

The concluding prayer indicates that a bishop is minister of the word in doctrine and deed who serves God and the congregation.

'Almighty God, giver of all good things, which by your holy spirit has appointed diverse orders of ministers in thy Church: mercifully behold this your servant, now called to the work and ministry of a Bishop, and replenish him so with the truth of your doctrine, and innocence of life, that both by word and deed, he may faithfully serve you in this office, to the glory of your name, and profit of your congregation.'

The public examination of the bishop-elect differed from Sarum in a very important omission: there was no examination of the candidate's faith and doctrine concerning the sacrament of the altar. The examination emphasized the bishop's appointment to *govern* the congregation.

'Forasmuch as holy scripture and the old Canons command, that we should not be hasty in laying on hands and admitting of any person to the government of the congregation of Christ, which he has purchased with no less price than the effusion of his own blood; before that I admit you to this administration whereunto you are called, I will examine you in certain articles, to the end the congregation present, may have a trial and bear witness how you be minded to behave yourself in the church of God.

Are you persuaded that you be truly called to this ministration according to the will of our Lord Jesus Christ, and the order of this realm?'

The examination also emphasized the sufficiency of scripture, justification by faith, and the bishop's office of teaching, exhortation and confutation of 'gainsaiers.'

'Will you then faithfully exercise yourself in the said holy scriptures, and call upon God by prayer for the true understanding of the same, so as you may be able by them to teach and exhort with wholesome doctrine, and to withstand and convince the gainsaiers?

Answer: I will so do, by the help of God.'

Again it is emphasized that the bishop is to be diligent in repudiating false doctrines and in encouraging others to do the same.

'Be you ready with all faithful diligence, to banish and
drive away all erroneous and strange doctrine, contrary
to God's word, and both privately and openly to call upon,
and encourage others to the same?

Answer: I am ready, the Lord being my helper.'

This ministry of leadership and teaching is emphasized once
again in the examination of a bishop's intention to live a godly
life, and his intention to lead and teach by example as well as
word.

'Will you deny all ungodliness and worldly lusts, and live
soberly, righteously, and godly in this world, that you
may show yourself in all things an example of good works
unto others, that the adversary may be ashamed, having
nothing to lay against you?

Answer: I will so do, the Lord being my helper.'

A final question signified a traditional role of the bishop
extending back to apostolic times, service of the poor and needy.

'Will you show yourself gentle, and be merciful for Christ's
sake to poor and needy people, and to all strangers desti-
tute of help?

Answer: I will so show myself by God's help.'

After a hymn to the Holy Spirit 'as it is set out in the order of
priests' there was a preface to the rite of consecration. The
preface teaches that men are reconciled to God through the
merits of Christ; it recalls the diversity of gifts within the
church, 'some Apostles, some Prophets, some Evangelists, some
Pastors and doctors, to the edifying and making perfect of his
congregation', it portrays the bishop as one who teaches, governs
and serves the people committed to him.

'Grant we beseech you, to this your servant such grace,
that he may be evermore ready to spread abroad thy
gospel, and glad tidings of reconcilement to God, and to
use the authority given unto him, not to destroy, but to
save, not to hurt, but to help: so that he as a wise and a
faithful servant, giving to your family meat in due season,
may at the last day be received into joy, through Jesus
Christ our lord.'

The elect was then consecrated through imposition of hands and prayer as follows.

> 'Then the Archbishop and Bishops present, shall lay their hands upon the head of the elect Bishop, the Archbishop saying,
>
> Take the holy ghost, and remember that you stir up the grace of God, which is in you, by imposition of hands: for God has not given us the spirit of fear, but of power, and love, and of soberness.'

The archbishop placed the bible on the new bishop's neck with the following admonition.

> 'Give heed unto reading, exhortation and doctrine. Think upon these things contained in this book, be diligent in them, that the increase coming thereby, may be manifest unto all men. Take heed unto yourself, and unto teaching, and be diligent in doing them, for by doing this you shall save yourself, and them that hear you: through Jesus Christ our Lord.'

The newly consecrated bishop then accepted the pastoral staff, a ceremony which signified that he was the representative of the good shepherd, to feed his flock, to strengthen the weak, to serve the sick and suffering, and to reconcile the sinner.

> 'Be to the flock of Christ a shepherd, not a wolf: feed them, devour them not; hold up the weak, heal the sick, bind together the broken, bring again the outcasts, seek the lost. Be so merciful, that you be not too remiss, so minister discipline, that you forget not mercy; that when the chief shepherd shall come, you may receive the immarcescible crown of glory, through Jesus Christ our lord. Amen.'

Unlike the Sarum consecration rite the Ordinal provided that the newly consecrated bishop should receive Communion at the main service. At the end of the Lord's Supper the presiding archbishop invoked God's blessing on his servant that he might excel in his ministry of the word.

> 'Most merciful father, we beseech you to send down upon this your servant, your heavenly blessing, and so endue him with your holy spirit, that he preaching your word, may not only be earnest to reprove, beseech, and rebuke

with all patience and doctrine, but also may be to such as believe, an wholesome example in word, in conversation, in love, in faith, in chastity, and purity, that faithfully fulfilling his course, at the latter day he may receive the crown of righteousness, laid up by the Lord, the righteous judge, who lives and reigns, one God with the father and holy ghost, world without end. Amen.'

Not just this final collect but the entire preceeding rite stressed the bishop's ministry of the word in preaching, correction and example. His order differed from the priesthood in the *authority* he had received. Therefore Cranmer retained the rite of presentation of the pastoral staff. But the other paraphernalia used in the Sarum rite, save only surplice and cope, were considered expendable. This return to biblical simplicity was in accord with the Ordinal's emphasis that authority was service. It also accorded with the Ordinal's omission of every reference to the high priesthood. The Sarum examination of the elect, which included all the major dogmas of the church including the traditional faith in the eucharist, was omitted. In the Ordinal there was no mention of sacerdotal grace, no Aaronic typology, no mention of high priestly robes, no unction of head and hands with prayers which mentioned the power of consecration. Equally significant is the fact that the new bishop did not preside at an episcopal Mass but 'communicated' with the archbishop.

The 1550 Ordinal was more than a liturgical repristination. In its omissions and emphases it signified what it was intended to convey — a reformed ministry differing from that in which the old church believed and which was signified and conveyed in the pontifical. Because the Ordinal was more than a liturgical revision and because it did far more that prune rites and prayers susceptible of superstition it was not welcomed by the old church. Nor was it really satisfactory to protestants for whom Cranmer never went far enough. Cranmer listened not to Rome but to the reformers' criticism of his new liturgy. He weighed their comments and, in some cases, their invective and, in 1552, brought forth a drastically revised Communion Service and a slightly but significantly revised Ordinal.

Reactions to the 1550 Ordinal

Especially where the liturgy was concerned, the charged theological atmosphere in the closing months of Edward's (and Cranmer's) reign was not conducive to dispassionate discussion. Among the aspects of public prayer about which feelings were especially strong were vestments and their meaning. The archbishop of Canterbury, as we have seen, retained some vestments in the new Ordinal. His position on vestments is articulated clearly in the treatise on ceremonies in the *Book of Common Prayer*. Cranmer reasoned that vestments conducive to God's glory and popular edification should be retained — even if they first came into use after the era of the primitive church; vestments (such as the chasuble) which had been abused or become otiose should be discarded. Cranmer sincerely believed that the minimal vestments he retained in the Communion Service and Ordinal were conducive to devotion.

> 'For we think it convenient that every country should use such ceremonies, as they shall think best to the setting forth of God's honour or glory, and to the reducing of the people to a most perfect and godly living, without error or superstition: and that they should put away other things, which from time to time they perceive to be most abused, as in men's ordinances it often chanceth diversely in diverse countries.' [13]

Martin Bucer's attitude towards vestments was similar to Cranmer's; the Strasbourg reformer wished vestments eliminated from the Communion Service because, in his opinion, their retention was conducive to superstition, 'not because I believe there is anything objectively wrong in them so that instructed men are unable to use them ordinately, but I see they are a cause of superstition to many.' [14] Peter Martyr, as seems clear from a letter Martyr wrote to Henry Bullinger, agreed with Bucer: '... since that diversity of apparel possesses little or no

---

[13] *The Two Liturgies in the Reign of Edward VI*, Joseph Ketley, ed., Cambridge, 1844, p. 199.

[14] 'Censura Martini Buceri super libro sacrorum seu ordinationis Ecclesiae atque ministerii in regno Angliae', in *Scripta Anglicana*, Basle, 1577, p. 458.

edification and very many persons superstitiously abuse it, I therefore considered that it ought to be removed. Bucer made very nearly the same answer....' [15]

A more vehement and implacable critic of vestments at the eucharist and in the ordering of ministers was John Hooper. Against Hooper's will the Edwardine Council appointed him bishop of Gloucester. Hooper adamantly refused either to swear by the saints or to wear vestments at his consecration. After a year of intransigence on both sides Council agreed to accept the oath of Supremacy from Hooper without mention of the saints and evangelists. But they insisted that the vestments rubrics in the Ordinal be used at Hooper's consecration. As Micronius wrote to Bullinger in 1550, 'they are all of them intent upon subjecting Hooper to their ceremonies, so he opposes them with all his might, and refers every thing to the apostolic ceremonies'. [16] After protracted wrangling Hooper was unceremoniously committed to the Fleet. Under this duress Hooper relented but, even then, won the concession that on most formal occasions he would not have to wear vestments in his diocese. [17]

The rationale of Hooper's animus towards vestments was a preview of the Puritan argument in the Elizabethan vestment controversy: only those ceremonies clearly enjoined in scripture were in accord with the word of God. Hooper thought vestments were a human accretion which, obscuring the unique mediation of Christ, fomented superstition about the mass and priesthood. [18] 'He that will be admitted to the ministry of God's word or his sacraments, must come in white vestments, which seemeth to repugn plainly with the former doctrine that confessed the only word of God to be sufficient. [19]

---

[15] Peter Martyr to Henry Bullinger, Oxford, January 28, 1551, in *Original Letters,* Vol II, pp. 487-488; cf. John Burcher to Bullinger, Strasbourg, December 28, 1550, *Ibid.,* p. 675.

[16] Martin Micronius to Henry Bullinger, London, October 13, 1550, *Ibid.,* p. 571.

[17] John Foxe, *Acts and Monuments,* Vol. VI, pp. 640-641.

[18] Micronius to Bullinger, *Original Letters,* Vol. II, p. 571.

[19] 'The Third Sermon Upon Jonas', in *Early Writings of John Hooper,* Samuel Carr, ed., Cambridge, 1848, p. 488.

Cranmer listened to these criticisms. He believed his original Ordinal was in conformity with scripture and the primitive church and that it conveyed the pure ministry of word and sacraments. But he refined his Ordinal still further to satisfy critics such as John Hooper and the more moderate Martin Bucer.

THE ORDINAL OF 1552

After the fall of Protector Somerset a revised edition of the *Book of Common Prayer* and the Ordinal was discussed cursorily in Convocation and at length in parliament. [20] Accordingly a Second Act of Uniformity was passed and took effect on All Saints day, 1 November, 1552. For the remaining months of Edward VI's reign the second *Book of Common Prayer* was the only authorized form of worship. The prescribed liturgies, especially the Communion Service, were decidedly more protestant than the 1549 rites. [21] The lament of Brother Giles was paraphrased to read 'Geneva, Geneva, thou hast destroyed Rome'. Cranmer and Council knew their Englishmen. Most citizens, clergy and laity alike, were prepared like the future vicar of Bray to accept changes providing these changes did not disrupt their daily lives. In 1552 they accepted, where it was put in use, a more protestant Prayer Book than they had previously known.

Cranmer's modifications of the Ordinal were not as extensive as in the Communion Service. But they were important; for they refined still further the Ordinal's signification of a ministry of word and sacrament which excluded eucharistic sacrifice. Cranmer preserved intact the Preface which expressed the Ordinal's purpose — to continue the apostolic ministry of bishop, priest and deacon in the Church of England. There was however, a slight but significant change in the introductory rubric for the ordering of deacons. Hooper and other extremists had

---

[20] Procter and Frere, *A New History of the Book of Common Prayer*, pp. 80-81.

[21] Edward P. Echlin, *The Anglican Eucharist in Ecumenical Perspective*, pp. 66-88.

protested about the use of vestments as unscriptural and conducive to the superstition of propitiatory sacrifice. In the 1550 Ordinal deacons were to be vested 'in a plain alb'. Cranmer omitted this requirement in 1552.

In the ordination form for priests the rubric that candidates were presented, 'every one of them having upon him a plain alb' was omitted. The most important alteration in the 1552 Ordinal occurred at the transmission of instruments. For in 1550 Cranmer had retained the important medieval addition to the ordination rite albeit with an altered formula. The protestant reformers objected that this rite was still patent of sacrificial interpretation. Cranmer responded by pruning the medieval ceremony still further. The changed ceremony of 1552, especially when compared side by side with its predecessor, is important in any assessment of the native character and spirit of the Ordinal. Because of the importance of the 1552 alteration the two ceremonies are juxtaposed here.

1550	1552
'The Bishop shall deliver to every one of them, the Bible in the one hand, and the Chalice or cup with the bread, in the other hand, and saying.	'The bishop shall deliver to every one of them the Bible in his hand, saying.
Take thou authority to preach the word of God, and to minister the holy Sacraments in this congregation, where thou shall be so appointed.'	Take thou authority to preach the word of God, and to minister the holy Sacraments in this congregation, where thou shall be so appointed.'

The transmission of the bible alone without the accompanying cup and bread signified what the authors of the Ordinal intended this ceremony to signify — a ministry of word and sacrament but not the power of consecration and sacrifice. The omission of the eucharistic instruments is a clear instance of where an omission is more indicative of the rite's intended signification than what was retained. Although the preface clearly states the authors' intent to continue the triadic ministry, their omissions of ceremonies which in the Pontifical signified sacrifice betrays a different understanding of apostolic ministry than that of the adherents of the old church. What seems clear from these omissions, especially the omission of the tradition of cup and bread in 1552, is that the framers of the Ordinal did not wish their rite to connote priestly sacrifice.

This intention is evident in the few changes made in the rite for consecration of bishops. In 1552 the rubric that the elect and his presenting bishops should be vested in surplice and cope 'having their pastoral staves in their hand' was omitted. The oath of obedience did not conclude, as it had in 1550, with 'so help me God, and his holy gospel' but with the words 'so help me God through Jesus Christ'. The consecrating bishop did not as in 1550 lay the bible on the neck of the new bishop but, in the words of the 1552 rubric, 'shall deliver him the Bible'. Finally, the rite of tradition of the pastoral staff was omitted. These changes placated critics who objected to certain ceremonies in the 1550 rite as non-biblical and who wished the rite to signify more clearly the unique priesthood and mediation of Christ.

Conclusion

With the distribution of the second *Book of Common Prayer* in the late autumn of 1552 Thomas Cranmer's liturgical reforms were virtually complete. His liturgy — and his episcopacy — were destined to be operative for only a few more months. Only one bishop is known to have been consecrated according to Cranmer's second Ordinal in contrast to the five by the first. With the death of Edward VI and the accession of Mary Tudor the Mass replaced the Communion Service, the pontifical replaced the Ordinal, and Reginald Pole was nominated to replace Cranmer himself. [22] But the Marian interlude was brief. The Edwardine Ordinal was soon in use in England again and has influenced all subsequent Anglican ordination rites.

---

[22] W.H. Frere, *The Marian Reaction*, London, 1896, p. 90.

CHAPTER V

Between two Restorations: Mary to Charles II

'The Ordinal was under the notice of the Pope and Cardinals from the early autumn of 1553.'

T.A. Lacey

As the brief Marian restoration began the traditional rites (even before they were officially authorized) were used in places where the old faith was strong. Julius Terentianus described the scene at Oxford, 'The papists, who had been always longing for this most wished-for day, dig out as it were from their graves their vestments, chalices and portasses.' [1]

Queen Mary herself moved cautiously. At first Mass was legal only in royal chapels and the universities. But on 14 September, 1553, Cranmer went to the Tower for his utterances against the Mass. On 20 December the royal Act of Repeal of the Edwardine settlement restored the situation to that of Henry VIII. [2] Late in 1554 a second Act of Repeal restored

---

[1] Julius Terentianus to Henry Bullinger, *Original Letters*, Vol. I, p. 369.

[2] H. Gee and W. Hardy, *Documents Illustrative of English Church History*, p. 379.

communion with Rome. [3] The pontifical was again in use for
ordinations but there was still confusion about the status of
ministers ordained with other rites or by bishops not duly
consecrated.

For some months Ordinal priests continued to administer
the sacraments and enjoy benefices. [4] By March, 1554, the
Ordinal bishops had been deposed but the Queen's directive
to Stephen Gardiner and the Catholic bishops concerning the
depositions says nothing about the Ordinal or the nullity of the
consecration of Bishop Taylor of Lincoln who had remained
unmarried. [5] A prepared homily by restored Bishop Edmund
Bonner of London probably provides a clue to the reaction of
the Queen and her Catholic subjects to Ordinal ministers. The
ministry of men ordained with Cranmer's rite was deficient at
best because they had not received the power to consecrate and
offer the eucharist. In Bonner's words which were read from
the pulpits in his diocese,

> 'The late-made ministers in the time of the schism, in their
> new devised ordination, having no authority at all given
> them to offer in the Mass the body and blood of our
> Saviour Christ, but both they so ordered (or rather dis-
> ordered) and their schismatical orderers also, utterly
> despising and impugning not only the oblation or sacrifice
> of the Mass, but also the real presence of the body and
> blood of our Saviour Christ in the sacrament of the altar,
> therefore I say, that all such both damnably and presump-
> tuously did offend against almighty God, and also most
> pitifully beguiled the people of this realm, who by this
> means were defrauded of the most blessed body and blood
> of our Saviour Christ, and the most comfortable fruit
> thereof and also of the sacrifice of the Mass, and of the
> inestimable fruit which cometh thereby . . .' [6]

In his visitation articles of September 1554, Bonner again
referred to *Ordinal* ministers as 'schismatics', the same epithet

---

[3] *Ibid.*, p. 382.

[4] J.J. Hughes, *Absolutely Null and Utterly Void*, pp. 252-253.

[5] Burnet, *History of the Reformation*, Vol. V, p. 388.

[6] Edmund Bonner, 'Of the Sacrament of Orders', in *A Profitable and
Necessary Doctrine*, London, 1554, no pagination.

which he applied to *married* priests. However, neither in his homily nor in his injunction does Bonner state flatly and un-equivocally that men ordained with the Ordinal are not ministers *at all* because they were ordained with a rite incapable of conveying Christian ministry. But his language is strong indeed.

> 'Whether any such as were ordered schismatical, and contrary to the old order and custom of the Catholic Church, or being unlawfully and schismatically married, after the late innovation and manner, being not yet recon-ciled nor admitted by the ordinary, have celebrated or said, either Mass or other divine service, within any cure or place of this city or diocese?' [7]

In 1550 Stephen Gardiner objected to the Ordinal's omission of unction; but he did not say the rite was incapable of making priests. [8] Later in a sermon before the Queen and Pole in 1554 he scored those so ordained as 'lay, profane and married'. [9] Gardiner required degree candidates at Cambridge, where he was again Chancellor, to subscribe to an article that is more apposite than his sermon. According to the article some ministers lacked power to consecrate and offer Christ's body and blood. 'The power of consecrating the body and blood of Christ has been granted only to priests lawfully ordained by Christ accord-ing to the rite of the Catholic Church.' [10]

In March 1554 the Queen issued injunctions concerning religion. Included is the phrase that her newly appointed bishops are to supply what is wanting in men ordained 'according to the new sort and fashion of order'. The Queen states that these men are 'not ordered in very deed.'

> 'Touching such persons as were heretofore promoted to any Orders, after the new sort and fashion of order, con-sidering that they were not ordered in very deed, the bishop of the diocese finding otherwise sufficiency and ability in these men, may supply that thing which wanted in them

[7] Burnet, *The History of the Reformation,* Vol. V, pp. 388-389.
[8] *Supra,* pp. 27-28.
[9] *Epistolarum Reginaldi Pole,* Part I, p. 256.
[10] Quoted in Darwell Stone, *A History of the Doctrine of the Holy Eucharist,* 2 Vols., London, 1909, Vol. II, p. 163.

before and then, according to his discretion, admit them
to minister.' [11]

It seems safe to conclude that the Queen and her bishops
believed something was lacking in those ordered with the Ordinal
or other reformed rites. They acted on this conviction by reordaining Ordinal ministers when these men desired to continue
in the active ministry and were judged worthy to do so. After
studying some of the records of reordinations the late Walter
Frere concluded, 'that the second ordination was in most cases
not a supplying of any supposed defects in the first but a real
re-ordination, implying an entire disbelief on the part of some-
one in the validity of the Edwardine Ordinal.' [12]

Commenting on the evidence for reordination of those
ordained with the Ordinal, Francis Clark states that Catholic
authorities 'deliberately and definitely' rejected Edwardine orders
as 'invalid'.

> 'There is indeed abundant evidence from many inde-
> pendent sources showing plainly that in Mary's reign the
> Catholic authorities, both in England and Rome, deli-
> berately and definitely rejected as invalid the ordinations
> which had been performed in the previous reign by use
> of the new English rite.' [13]

There is indeed evidence of at least sixteen reordinations during
the Marian restoration.

In the words of Queen Mary's injunction reordinations were
meant to 'supply that thing which wanted in them before'. [15]

Roman authorities also found Edwardine orders wanting. In
July, 1553, Pope Julius III authorized Reginald Pole to dispense
ministers from irregularities 'provided that before their lapse
they had been rightfully and lawfully promoted or ordained';

---

[11] Burnet, *History of the Reformation,* Vol. V., p. 385.

[12] Frere, *The Marian Reaction,* p. 121.

[13] Francis Clark, *The Catholic Church and Anglican Orders,* London,
1962, p. 14.

[14] Frere, *The Marian Reaction,* p. 203; cf. Francis Clark, *Eucharistic
Sacrifice and the Reformation,* p. 204.

[15] *Supra,* p. 117.

those not so promoted, providing they were repentant and worthy, 'might now be promoted to all the orders, including sacred orders and the priesthood'. [16] The Pope therefore had doubts about the orders of men 'promoted' under Edward VI. Similarly, Pope Paul IV in *Praeclara carissimi* and *Regimini universalis* of 1555 expressed doubts about the consecration of some bishops and therefore about the orders of all those ordained by those bishops. Cardinal Pole seems to have provided for the 'promotion' to orders of deacons and priests ordained with the Ordinal. The Pope went beyond this by legislating for men who may have been ordered with a satisfactory rite but by a *bishop* not *rite et recte ordinatus*.

> 'Only those Bishops and Archbishops who were not ordained and consecrated in the form of the Church cannot be said to have been validly and lawfully ordained. Hence those persons promoted by them to those Orders have not received Orders, but ought and are bound to receive the said Orders anew.' [17]

The Pope added that men ordained by bishops consecrated 'in the form of the church' had received the character of the orders bestowed. The Pope does not say, but seems to presume, that the bishops ordain others 'in the form of the church'.

> 'Those on whom Orders of this kind were conferred by Bishops and Archbishops who were themselves ordained and consecrated in the form of the Church — even though these Bishops and Archbishops were schismatics and received the churches over which they preside in former times from the hand of Henry VIII and Edward VI, pretended kings of England — have received the character of those Orders which were bestowed on them.' [18]

The Pope approved of Pole's policies in restoring England to the Roman communion including his dispensations for the ordination of Edwardine clerics 'that they may be promoted to orders and benefices obtained invalidly under the schism'. [19] It

---

[16] In C. Hoare, *The Edwardine Ordinal,* Bristol, 1957, p. 35.

[17] Translation by J.J. Hughes in *Absolutely Null and Utterly Void,*

[18] *Ibid.*   [p. 261.

[19] From Pole's summary of his actions of which the Pope approved. Quoted in Hoare, *The Edwardine Ordinal,* p. 30.

is also noteworthy that condemned heretics were degraded from orders received with the pontifical but *not* from those with the Ordinal. [20]

In brief there is a convergence of evidence that Catholic authorities in the 16th century were at best dubious about orders administered with the Ordinal or by bishops not 'rite et recte' consecrated. And from Bonner's and Gardiner's words it seems what authorities found wanting was the power to conse- crate and offer Mass. But all parties were eager for the swift reintegration of the Church of England into the Catholic fold. The practice generally adopted seems to have been reordination of men whose orders were suspect but who otherwise possessed the desires and qualities for continuation in the ministry. [21]

Faced with a variety of ordinations and ministers and motivated by desire for restoration of full communion Catholic authorities neither asked nor answered the questions about ministry that were asked in later centuries. Their policy was a practical one for their own situation. It would be an error to assume that policy is a norm for different ages in different situations.

The Elizabethan Ordinal

The Elizabethan religious settlement was substantially politi- cal and therefore a compromise settlement. [22] Elizabeth was unable to restore religion as her father had left it for several reasons. [23] At first she lacked bishops. All the Marian prelates save one (Kitchen of Llandaff) stood firm and were deposed. In addition the Queen was more dependent on parliament than her father had been — and parliament was protestant. [24] More-

---

[20] John Foxe, *Acts and Monuments*, Vol. VI, p. 652.
[21] Clark, *Eucharistic Sacrifice and the Reformation*, p. 204.
[22] Neville Williams, *Elizabeth Queen of England*, London, 1967, pp. 67-68; John Hurstfield, 'Church and State: 1558-1615' in *Studies in Church History*, G.J. Cuming, ed., London, 1965, pp. 124-125.
[23] G.R. Elton, *England Under the Tudors*, London, 1965, pp. 263-266.
[24] *Ibid.*, p. 270.

over, because the Queen could not abide John Knox and the Geneva exiles she was obliged to collaborate with the Coxians from Frankfort who were protestants.

In an Act of Uniformity Elizabeth restored the 1552 Prayer Book with some changes. Despite subsequent doubts as to whether the Ordinal was included the Act seemingly provided for ordinations under the Ordinal in obliging the clergy to 'celebration of the Lord's Supper and administration of each of the sacraments, and all their common and open prayer, in such order and form as it is mentioned in the said fifth and sixth years of the reign of Edward VI'. [25]

There were later qualms about whether or not the Ordinal technically was a part of the second Prayer Book. [26] But in subsequent acts the Queen, parliament and convocation confirmed that ordination with the Ordinal was part of the settlement. [27]

The Queen's initial preference was for the Communion Service of 1549. [28] But as we have seen she had to work with former continental exiles and with a protestant parliament. There would be no going back root and branch to the second year of her brother's reign, much less to her father's settlement. The Queen, Cecil and the protestants agreed to a compromise Communion Service for the 1559 Prayer Book that included three significant changes in the direction of the 1549 Service. These three concessions won by the Queen are significant for the Ordinal and its signification, presuming that the Ordinal was part of the settlement. The first was an inclusion of the vestments rubric which had been deleted in 1552, thus beginning

---

[25] An Act for the Uniformity of Common Prayer and Service in the Church and Administration of the Sacraments, in Henry Gee, *The Elizabethan Clergy*, Oxford, 1898, p. 23.

[26] Hughes, *Absolutely Null and Utterly Void.*, p. 17.

[27] Cf. the rite for deacons and priests, printed in 1559, in *Liturgies and Occasional Forms of Prayer Set Forth in the Reign of Queen Elizabeth*, William Keating Clay, ed., Cambridge, 1846, pp. 272-298. Cf. J.E. Neale, *Elizabeth I and Her Parliaments*, 2 Vols., London, 1953, Vol. I, p. 83.

[28] Neale, *Elizabeth I and Her Parliaments*, p. 78.

I

the long and fateful vestments controversy. [29] That the reversion
to 1549 was a compromise interpreted differently by different
factions appears in an interesting letter of Edmund Sandys to
Matthew Parker who, as Archbishop of Canterbury, was to be
involved in controversy over the Queen's predilection for vestments and images.

> 'The last book of service is gone through with a proviso
> to retain the ornaments which were used in the first and
> second year of King Edward until it please the Queen to
> take order for them. Our gloss upon this text is, that we
> shall not be forced to use them, but that others in the
> meantime shall not convey them away, but that they may
> remain for the Queen. [30]

A second adjustment concerned the 'black rubric' which Cranmer
had appended to the 1552 Communion Service. This was
dropped in 1559. The rubric which King and Council, en-
couraged by Elizabeth's nemesis John Knox, had goaded
Cranmer into composing professed that a kneeling reception,

> 'is not meant thereby, that any adoration is done, or ought
> to be done, either to the Sacramental bread or wine there
> bodily received, or to any real and essential presence there
> being of Christ's natural flesh and blood. For as concerning
> the Sacramental bread and wine, they remain still in their
> very natural substances, and therefore may not be adored,
> for that were Idolatry to be abhorred of all faithful chris-
> tians. And as concerning the natural body and blood of
> our saviour Christ, they are in heaven and not here: for
> it is against the truth of Christ's true natural body, to be
> in more places than in one at one time.' [31]

The omission of this rubric left room for a more comprehensive
doctrine of the true and real presence and therefore of the
priest's role at the eucharist than had the 1552 Service.

---

[29] *Ibid.*, p. 29. Cf. *Elizabethan Puritanism,* Leonard Trinterus, ed.,
N.Y., 1971, pp. 61-71.

[30] Edward Sandys to Matthew Parker, 30 April, 1559, *The Corres-
pondence of Matthew Parker,* John Bruce, ed., Cambridge, 1848,
p. 65.

[31] Echlin, *The Anglican Eucharist in Ecumenical Perspective,* p. 88.

The third change involved the formula for distribution of communion. In 1549 Cranmer's formula had been conservative and patent of a 'realist' doctrine of the presence. In 1552 he substituted a severely receptionist formula. In a stroke of comprehensiveness Elizabeth and the protestants juxtaposed both formulas in 1559. The Elizabethan communion formula therefore read as follows,

> 'Then shall the minister first receive the Communion in both kinds himself, and next deliver it to other ministers, if any be there present (that they may help the chief minister,) and after to the people in their hands kneeling. And when he delivers the bread he shall say,
>
> The body of our Lord Jesus Christ, which was given for thee, preserve thy body and soul into everlasting life; and take and eat this in remembrance that Christ died for thee, and feed on him in thine heart by faith, with thanksgiving.
>
> And the minister that delivereth the cup, shall say,
>
> The blood of our Lord Jesus Christ, which was shed for thee, preserve thy body and soul into everlasting life; and drink this in remembrance that Christ's blood was shed for thee, and be thankful.' [32]

These changes in the Communion Service reflected and influenced belief. In calling attention to them we are reiterating what has been said earlier in these pages — that a church's faith can determine the signification of an ordination rite. In other words, a church is not bound for all time to the signification intended for a rite by its primordial framers and users; a community's developing faith, doctrine and theology, can and does influence the meaning of its liturgy: *lex credendi est lex orandi*. [33] Refusal to acknowledge this principle is an underlying weakness in Francis Clark's lucid and logical discussion of the form of the Ordinal. [34]

---

[32] *Ibid.*, pp. 93-94.

[33] Yves Congar, 'Liturgy, Principal Instrument of the Church's Tradition', in *Yves Congar, O.P.*, Martin Redfern, ed., London, 1972, pp. 99-101.

[34] Francis Clark, *Anglican Orders and Defect of Intention*, pp. 168-191.

The Uniformity Act of 1559 provides for 'each of the sacraments . . . in such order and form as it is mentioned in the said fifth and sixth year of the reign of Edward VI'. Elizabeth, believing she now had an Ordinal, began the search for consecrators of her choice as Archbishop of Canterbury, Matthew Parker.

But fifteen of the remaining sixteen diocesans were deposed. This meant the Queen had an anomalous situation confronting her. She and parliament desired a peaceful, legal and secure continuance of the hierarchy. Although the settlement and the succession were as much political as religious the settlement demanded continuation of the historic episcopate.

Parker was nominated in the summer of 1559. In December the Queen issued letters patent for his consecration, addressing them to Kitchen, Barlow, bishop-elect of Chichester, Scory, bishop-elect of Hereford, Coverdale, formerly bishop of Exeter, Bale, bishop of Ossory, and suffragan bishops Hodgkin and Salisbury. Any four were to confirm the election by the chapter of Canterbury and, then, consecrate the elect. Clearly this was an unprecedented procedure. Therefore the Queen added her 'supplentes' clause, supplying for whatever might be lacking in the persons of the consecrators or in legality.

Parker's election was confirmed at St Mary-le-Bow by his four future consecrators: Barlow, Scory, Coverdale and Hodgkin. Barlow and Hodgkin had been consecrated with the pontifical under Henry VIII; Scory and Coverdale in 1551 by pontifical bishops using the first Ordinal. At Lambeth chapel, 17 December, 1559, all four said the form over Parker using the 1552 Ordinal. It is interesting to notice that Parker, Scory and Hodgkin wore surplices; Barlow, the principal consecrator, a silk cope; Coverdale, a long woolen gown. [35]

Four days later Parker and three of his consecrators consecrated three bishops with the 1552 Ordinal. The succession was continued in England. The evidence for Parker's own consecration has always been good and is now almost universally conceded. And as we have just seen there were pontifical bishops

---

[35] J.J. Hughes, *Absolutely Null and Utterly Void*, pp. 13-17.

among Parker's own consecrators who, through Parker, may be found in the genealogy of most Anglican bishops. Once these facts were admitted by Roman Catholics the controversy about Anglican ministry focused not on whether or not Parker was ritually consecrated but on the Ordinal and the intention of those who first used it.

The Queen's 'supplentes' clause issued before Parker's consecration was to supply anything *legally* wanting in the re-institution of the Ordinal. The entire process was carefully recorded and the consecration itself is carefully described in the Lambeth register. [36] Despite the frail legality of Parker's unusual consecration there is, through Parker and his consecrators, at the very least a tactile link with the old hierarchy.

Another Tudor prelate worthy of notice is the Elizabethan bishop of Dublin, Hugh Curwen. Curwen was consecrated by Edmund Bonner 8 September, 1555, at St Paul's with the pontifical. He served as bishop of Dublin under Mary and Elizabeth until 1567 when he was translated to Oxford where he died in 1568. Curwen participated in several consecrations during the first decade of Elizabeth's reign, and his name appears in Laud's table of consecration. William Laud, later archbishop of Canterbury, like Parker, is in the genealogy of most present Anglican bishops. [37] Through Curwen who was consecrated by pontifical bishops themselves using the pontifical there is another link of the Anglican hierarchy with the pontifical succession.

But such niceties did not engage the majority of Elizabethans. The majority of the faithful conformed to the most recent change in religion; accepted their vicars and curates whether they were ordained by the pontifical, pontifical bishops or by pastors themselves consecrated by Ordinal bishops using the

---

[36] E.E. Estcourt, *The Question of Anglican Ordinations Discussed,* London, 1873, p. 86; V.J.K. Brook, *A Life of Archbishop Parker,* Oxford, 1962, pp. 84-85.

[37] Hughes, *Absolutely Null and Utterly Void,* p. 24; for a brief description of Antonio de Dominis who also enters Laud's genealogy through de Dominis' consecration of George Monteigne who was one of Laud's four consecrators, cf. *Ibid.,* p. 25.

Ordinal. When the Elizabethan Ordinal was put into use there
had been four great changes in religion in twenty-two years
and numerous lesser tackings. Most Elizabethan Englishmen
both at home and in the Pale were content to get on with their
lives and to let ecclesiastics debate the fine points of ordination.

A minority, however, remained faithful to the old church
and sceptical about the new fashion of ordering which was done
without the customary form of the church. [38] Roman Catholic
spokesmen gradually focused their attack on the Ordinal's
numerous omissions of sacrificial symbolism. This more sophisti-
cated attack on Anglican ministry was accompanied by less
durable pamphleteering which impugned the consecration of
Barlow, Parker's principal consecrator, and the reality of Parker's
own consecration; it was alleged in the 'Nag's Head tale' that
Parker was 'consecrated' in a bogus ceremony in a Cheapside
tavern. [39] All of this had its effect on Catholics like Margaret
Taylor of York who 'cometh not to church because there is not
a priest as there ought to be, and also that there is not the
Sacrament of the Altar', and the daughter of Thomas Hewitt
who absented herself from church 'because there is no priest
there nor right sacrament'. [40]

But these sentiments were held by a minority. The majority
of Englishmen conformed. There were no more abrupt religious
changes under Elizabeth and when a new monarch, James I,
came to the throne there was, at long last, a new ruler *without*
a concomitant change in religion. The Ordinal was part of the
Jacobean settlement of 1604 — the Prayer Book and episcopacy
were to be maintained.

But there were omens of trouble to come. The Elizabethan
settlement had already rebuffed Puritan pleas that 'pastor' or

[38] Christopher Devlin, *The Life of Robert Southwell*, London, 1956, pp. 17-19.

[39] Hughes, *Absolutely Null and Utterly Void*, pp. 17-22.

[40] David Matthew, *Catholicism in England, 1535-1935*, London, 1936, p. 41; Cf. John Bossy, 'The Catholic Community of Yorkshire', 1558-1791; *The Ampleforth Journal*, Summer, 1973, pp. 27-33, esp. 27-30.

'minister' replace 'priest' in the liturgy. [41] The Puritans sent a petition to James requesting 'divers terms of priests and absolution and some other used, with the ring in marriage, and other such like in the book, may be corrected'. [42] The king provided the conference between representative puritan and episcopal divines at Hampton Court in 1604. Of the slight concessions granted the Puritans none pertained to the Ordinal. In a series of canons, the Jacobean settlement provided for a decent communion table suitably covered, a pulpit, a bible and an alms box in each church. These were connected indirectly with the Communion Service and Ordinal; but the liturgy itself remained virtually intact.

The 1662 Ordinal

From late in Elizabeth's reign there was a 'Catholic' reaction within the Church of England which attempted to recover the traditional concept of the eucharist as a representative memorial of Christ's sacrifice. The Laudians, as they were eventually called, had a predilection for the 1549 Communion Service. [43] In 1620 John Cosin prepared a book of devotions which included for private prayer at Mass parts of the 1549 Communion Service which had been eliminated by Cranmer in the more protestant service of 1552. Cosin also distinguished clearly between the three grades of the hierarchy and applied the biblical term 'pastor' to bishops. The distinction within the hierarchy and the appropriate use of titles such as pastor, vicar and curate were points at issue between the Laudians and the puritan party throughout the Stuart era and were to surface again when the Ordinal was next revised in 1662. [44]

In the year in which Cosin's *Collection of Private Devotions* appeared the Scottish bishops produced an Ordinal for ordaining

[41] Neale, *Elizabeth I and Her Parliaments,* Vol. I, p. 207.

[42] Millenary Petition, in *A History of Conferences and Other Proceedings Connected With the Revision of the Book of Common Prayer,* Edward Cardwell, ed., Oxford, 1849, p. 132.

[43] Articles to be Inquired of by the Churchwardens and Swornmen, *The Works of the Right Reverend Father in God, John Cosin,* 5 Vols., Oxford, 1845, Vol. II, p. 9.

[44] *Ibid.,* p. 304.

priests or 'ministers' and consecrating bishops but with no provision for the diaconate. [45] The Laudian faction in England urged a revision of the English Ordinal but without success. [46] The Laudians did co-operate with the Scottish bishops in the preparation of the Scottish Communion Service of 1637 which was rejected by the Scots. [47]

As episcopal and presbyterian positions hardened to the point where war was imminent a commission with representatives of both parties attempted in 1641 to reconcile their differences. The published 'Proceedings' included a phrase expressing Puritan objections to the Laudian preference for 'putting to the liturgy printed "secundo, tertio Edwardi Sexti", which the parliament both reformed and laid aside'. [48] Parliament was indeed destined to support Puritan aspirations for a time.

In 1645 the Book of Common Prayer was outlawed, the Directory, little more than an outline, became the authorized service book. The Ordinal was driven underground — and dangerously few ordinations took place. The episcopacy seemed for a time in danger of dying out as James Wedderburn of Scotland died, William Laud was executed, Matthew Wren went to the Tower, and John Cosin to exile in France.

Wren used his enforced leisure to prepare 'devices' for revision of the Prayer Book, convinced that 'never could there have been an opportunity so offenceless on the church's part for amending the Book of Common Prayer as now, when it hath been so long disused as not one in five hundred is so perfect in it as to observe alterations'. [49] In France John Cosin both familiarized himself with the presbyterian viewpoint and

---

[45] G.J. Cuming, *A History of Anglican Liturgy,* London, 1969, p. 143.

[46] *Ibid.,* p. 145.

[47] Gordon Donaldson, *The Making of the Scottish Prayer Book of 1637,* Edinburgh, 1954, pp. 49, 85.

[48] Proceedings of Some Worthy and Learned Divines Touching Innovations in the Doctrine and Discipline of the Church of England, Together with Considerations on the Common Prayer Book, in *A History of Conferences,* Cardwell, ed., p. 273.

[49] Matthew Wren, 'Advices' in *The Durham Book,* G.J. Cuming ed., London, 1961, pp. 287-288.

prepared for the eventual restoration and liturgical revision. When Charles II was invited to assume the throne Cosin drew up a list of 'particulars' for Prayer Book reform.

The presbyterian party desired a thorough review of the Book of Common Prayer including the use of 'pastor' or 'minister' for the parish priest. They requested of Charles,

> 'That each congregation may have a learned, orthodox and godly pastor residing amongst them, ... the Book of Common Prayer hath in it many things that are justly offensive and need amendment, hath been long discontinued and very many, both ministers and people, persons of pious, loyal and peaceful minds are therein greatly dissatisfied ... some learned, godly, and moderate divines of both persuasions, indifferently chosen, may be employed to compile such a form as is before described. ... ' [50]

The king promised freedom of conscience. His declaration seemed to imply toleration of non-conformists.

> 'We do again renew what we have formerly said in our declaration from Breda, for the liberty of tender consciences, that no man shall be disquieted or called in question for differences of opinion in matters of religion, which do not disturb the peace of the kingdom.' [51]

Charles responded to the presbyterian request for liturgical revision by convoking a conference at the Savoy. His warrant, however, betrayed a less tolerant stand than his previous declarations from Breda and Westminster. The government preference was for a return to the 1604 Prayer Book and the *status quo*. The king's warrant described the result of the conference in advance, ' ... avoiding as much as may be all unnecessary alterations of the forms and liturgy wherewith the people are already acquainted, and have so long received in the Church of England.' [52]

---

[50] Proposals of the Ministers, in *A History of Conferences,* pp. 279, 282.

[51] His Majesty's Declaration to All His Learned Subjects, *Ibid.,* p. 197; Maurice Ashley, *Charles II,* London, 1971, pp. 114-117.

[52] The Royal Warrant for the Conference at the Savoy, *A History of Conferences,* p. 300; David Ogg, *England in the Reign of Charles II,* 2 Vols., Oxford, 1934, Vol. I, pp. 152-153.

At the Savoy John Cosin was the intellectual leader of the Laudians, Richard Baxter of the non-conformists. [53] A Puritan sub-committee drew up a long list of 'execeptions' to the Prayer Book and Baxter, at the request of the episcopal party, quickly produced an alternative liturgy. The intransigent bishops conceded little. The temper of the government is indicated in the fact that the House of Commons in 1661 sent to the Lords an Act of Uniformity with the 1604 Prayer Book annexed. Neither Laudians nor presbyterians were to accomplish radical revision of the liturgy. However, the Puritan insistence on a virtual parity of ministers necessitated some clarification in the Ordinal. One of the Puritan 'exceptions' called for response: 'As the word "minister", and not priest or curate, is used in the Absolution, and in diverse other places; it may throughout the whole book be used instead of those two words.' [54]

The 'Durham Book' which contained the Laudian proposals did not provide for revision of the Ordinal. Therefore John Cosin used a 1634 edition to prepare a revision of the rite for deacons while Wren and William Sancroft revised the other rites. When the Laudian proposals were transcribed in the 1634 edition, with which Cosin had long been familiar, the resultant transcription became known as the 'Fair Copy'.

In general the temper of parliament remained inimical to extensive liturgical change and in favour of a new authorization of the 1604 Prayer Book with few alterations. Most Laudian recommendations for a return to the usages of 1549 or to the Scottish Prayer Book of 1637 were doomed. When parliament came to the Ordinal, however, the situation was different. Here both the government and the Laudians were at one in rejecting the presbyterian glosses on the Ordinal. Most of the Laudian recommendations for revision of the Ordinal carried. On 21 December 1661, the Book of Common Prayer, including a revised Ordinal, was signed by Convocation and annexed to an

[53] G.J. Cuming, *History of Anglican Liturgy*, p. 154.
[54] The Exceptions Against the Book of Common Prayer, *A History of Conferences*, pp. 307-308.

Act of Uniformity. [55] Royal assent was forthcoming 19 May 1662; the new Prayer Book was put in use on St Bartholomew's day.

The changes in the 1662 Ordinal countered the presbyterian position as voiced by Richard Baxter and reflected the views of John Cosin. To understand the new Ordinal's signification it is necessary to have some familiarity with the divergent teaching of Baxter and Cosin.

Richard Baxter, 'a meer Catholic'

Richard Baxter, the principal spokesman for the presbyterians in 1661, was a tolerant and moderate man, one who called himself 'a meer Catholic' and who in fact defies neat classification. Baxter's convictions before, during and after the restoration were clearly and courageously non-conformist. As a prolific and learned writer and preacher he was capable of holding his own with scholars such as Cosin and Wren and with political ecclesiastics such as Gilbert Sheldon. Baxter called himself a presbyterian who accepted episcopacy save only 'the English diocesan frame and all their impositions'. [56] He did not repudiate all episcopacy; but he did consistently object to the English diocesan system. For Baxter local ministers succeeded Christ and the apostles in the free power of governing as well as in teaching and sanctifying. He believed the diocesan system illicitly truncated the congregational ministry. If the restoration settlement granted 'episcopal' governing power to local ministers Baxter would have been willing to accept a bishopric. Because the restoration did *not* endorse his views Baxter declined promotion.

> 'I did not think that I should ever see cause to take any bishopric, but I could give no positive answer until I saw the king's resolution about the way of church government. For if the old diocesan frame continued, he knew we could never accept nor own it.' [57]

---

[55] Act of Uniformity, 1662, in *English Historical Documents*, 13 Vols., D. Douglas, ed., London, 1953, Vol. VIII, pp. 377-382.

[56] *Reliquiae Baxterianae*, J.M. Lloyd Thomas, ed., London, 1931, p. 154.

[57] *Ibid.*, p. 155.

According to Baxter priests and bishops did not differ in order
but in degree. The bishop governed, as first among equals, with
the consent and collaboration of presbyters. Baxter quoted with
approval an exposition of this theory of parity by Dr Reynolds
of Norwich.

> 'He read to me a profession directed to the king, which
> he had written wherein he professed that he took a bishop
> and presbyter to differ not *ordine* but *gradu*, and that a
> bishop was but the chief presbyter, and that he was not
> to ordain or govern but with his presbyters' assistance and
> consent.' [58]

Baxter acknowledged the desirability of episcopal ordinations for
good order; but he denied that bishops received a plenitude of
priesthood which lesser ministers did not share. Churches whose
ministers were ordained by presbyters were true churches and
their ministry should be recognized as such by the Church of
England.

> 'It was only the moderate ancient Episcopal party which I
> hoped for agreement with, it being impossible for the
> Presbyterian and Independent party to associate with them
> that take them and their churches, and all the reformed
> ministers and churches that have not episcopal ordination,
> for null. . .' [59]

Baxter did not defend a charismatic church order. In fact he
criticized the extreme independents for their lack of order. 'The
word of God is to be preached only by such as are sufficiently
gifted and also duly approved and called to that Office.' [60]

Aware of the ancient Celtic system in which bishops were
often under the jurisdiction of an abbot Baxter argued that these
ancestors of English bishops were not diocesan bishops in the

[58] *Ibid.,* p. 157; cf. I. Morgan, *The Non-Conformity of Richard
Baxter,* London, 1946, pp. 191-219.

[59] *Reliquiae Baxterianae,* p. 137; for Baxter's own ordination see the
balanced remarks of Geoffrey F. Nuttall in *Richard Baxter,* London,
1965, pp. 17-19.

[60] The Confession of Faith in *The Confession of Faith: Together
With the Larger and Lesser Catechisms Compared by the Reverend
Assembly of Divines then Sitting at Westminster,* London, 1688,
p. 312.

later unacceptable form. Moreover, he held that an ordination was not *absolutely* necessary for a man to be a minister or for a church to be a church. In times of necessity the ministry could be continued by recognition by the people of those who came forward as their ministers. In necessity the recognition by the community supplied what was lacking in the external appointment.

> 'If the way of regular ordination fail, God may otherwise (by the *Church's necessity* and *the notorious aptitude of the person*) notify his will to the Church, what person they shall receive (as if a layman were cast on the Indian shore, and converted thousands, who could have no ordination), and upon the people's reception or consent that man will be a true pastor.' [61]

Baxter himself was episcopally ordained and, after the Laudian restoration, defended his actions by testifying to his ordination and the licence of the diocesan bishop. 'I myself have the licence of the bishop of this diocese, as well as episcopal ordination.' [62]

But Baxter objected to the diocesan system as a corruption of evangelical and apostolic order. He argued that in the primitive church as established by Christ the local pastor — called vicar or rector by later ages — was the bishop of his flock with the ministry of leadership as well as teaching and sanctifying. In the English diocesan system the bishops usurped the office formerly held by archbishops and metropolitans and, moreover, truncated the office of presbyters by usurping their power to govern. At the restoration Baxter expected Charles II to restore what Baxter considered an *apostolic* hierarchy.

> 'By proving that the Covenant did not meddle against all bishops and archbishops, but only those of the English diocesan species; and that there was a specifical difference, I proved, in that by the king's Declaration the essentials at least of church-government are restored to the pastors, whereas before the pastors had no government.'

While Baxter was willing to accept a moderate and 'apostolic'

---

[61] *Reliquiae Baxterianae*, p. xxvi.
[62] *Ibid.*, p. 229.
[63] *Ibid.*, p. 158.

episcopal system, he was suspicious of the inherent tendency to
ambition and jealousy in the episcopacy as such.

> 'How excellent a man was Gregory Nazianzene, and
> highly valued in the church; and yet by reproach and
> discouragements driven away from his church at Con-
> stantinople, whither he was chosen; and envied by the
> bishops round about him. How worthy a man was the
> eloquent Chrysostome, and highly valued in the church;
> and yet how bitterly was he prosecuted by Hierome and
> Epiphanius; and banished, and died in a second banish-
> ment, by the provocation of factious contentious
> bishops.' [64]

By the true, apostolic episcopacy of the primitive church Baxter
meant the residential episcopacy as exemplified by Ignatius of
Antioch. Within a true and apostolic episcopal system the local
pastor would be the bishop within his congregation.

> 'They seem not to me to have taken the course which
> should have settled these distracted churches. Instead of
> disputing against all Episcopacy, they should have changed
> diocesan prelacy into such an Episcopacy as the conscience
> of the king might have admitted, and as was agreeable to
> that which the Church had in the two or three first
> ages.' [65]

Baxter sought to reconcile the episcopal and non-conformist
factions as one

> 'who like Ignatius's episcopacy, but not the English
> diocesan frame and like what is good in Episcopals,
> Presbyterians or Independents, but reject somewhat as
> evil in them all; being of the judgment which I have
> described myself to be in the beginning of this book.' [66]

Baxter thought episcopacy a useful development but not of
divine law. The diocesan system was not a legitimate development
but a corruption. *No* office has the prerogative to impose fixed
liturgies on other pastors.

---

[64] Richard Baxter, *The Divine Life,* 2 Vols., London, 1825, Vol. II,
pp. 248-249.
[65] *Reliquiae Baxterianae,* p. 62.
[66] *Ibid.,* p. 178.

'We never said it proved from scripture that Christ appointed any to such an office, as to make prayers for other pastors and churches to offer up to God: and this being none of the work of the apostolical, or common ministerial office in the Primitive Church, is no work of any office of Divine Institution.' [67]

In the primitive church the bishop was resident among his people and he enjoyed the necessary authority to lead them. Whether a community was called diocese or church or parish was indifferent to Baxter; but the pastor who leads the community must be physically *present*, he must understand the local situation *from within*, and he must have the power to act accordingly. Government by letter from the chancery was intolerable. The early 'churches' were like schools in which the teacher was present among those he taught. The diocesan system corrupted this until the pastor became a glorified usher and the bishop an absentee governor who ruled a hundred churches by letter. Baxter thought the restoration unchurched the parishes by making large dioceses the only 'churches' with 'pastors' who governed like distant Princes.

'You unchurch all our parish Churches. Every Church then had a bishop, no church now hath a Bishop (proper to itself), or at least not many. Therefore no Parish (by this rule) is a church. *Ecclesia est plebs Episcopo adunata.* You make no Church below a Diocese.' [68]

Royal appointment of bishops was unjustifiable by the criterion of the primitive church. The bishop should be elected by the clergy and people he serves. This was in fact the universal practice in East and West for hundreds of years until the Prince usurped the people's right to choose their bishop. 'He was to be taken as no Bishop who was chosen by Magistrates, Prelates or any, without the Clergy's election and the people's election

---

[67] *The Papers that Passed between the Commissioners Appointed by His Majesty for the Alteration of the Common Prayer, etc.,* London, 1665, p. 24.

[68] *Richard Baxter's Answer to Dr Edward Stillingfleet's Charge of Separation,* London, 1680, p. 79.

or consent: Christians then took not this to be any part of the Prince's trust.' [69]

Baxter could not conform to the Carolingian settlement. In his *Autobiography* he gave his reasons: the diocesan system was contrary to scripture; it usurped the royal power of pastors; it violated the hallowed principle of one bishop, one church; it subverted the discipline established by Christ; it gave the civil power prerogatives in the church that exceeded the powers of the sword.' [70]

In representing the presbyterian grievances Baxter was reluctant to endorse the use of 'priest' in the liturgy because, while it translated 'presbyter' and as such was tolerable, it was open to misunderstanding; the use of 'curate' was more misleading because it implied that pastors were functionaries not of the congregation but of the bishop.

> 'The word [Minister] may well be used instead of Priest and Curate, though the word [Deacon] for necessary distinction stand: yet we doubt not but [Priest] as it is but the English of Presbyter, is lawful: but it is from the common danger of mistake and abuse we argue. That all Pastors else are but the Bishop's Curates, is a doctrine that declares the heavy charge, and account of the Bishops and lends much to the ease of the Presbyters' minds, if it could be proved: if by [Curates] you mean such as have not directly by Divine Obligation the Cure of Souls, but only by the Bishops' delegation: But if the Office of a Presbyter be not of Divine Right: and so, if they be not the Curates of Christ, and Pastors of the Church, none are.' [71]

Despite Baxter's pervasive moderation he was a leading spokesman for a school of thought to which the Laudians and the government were opposed. Baxter's moderate position was, because of its very comprehensiveness, a threat to the dominant party. There was a real possibility that the doctrine he held could be read *into* the Ordinal. Baxter's theory of parity was

[69] *Ibid.*, p. 15; cf. pp. 27, 51.
[70] *Reliquiae Baxterianae*, pp. 180-186.
[71] *Papers That Passed Between the Commissioners*, pp. 68-69.

not accepted by many Laudians; and he deplored the diocesan system which they intended to restore.

The episcopacy Baxter favoured was not that endorsed by the Laudians. His theory of parity, of presbyteral government, and his avoidance of the word 'priest' jeopardized the clear gradation in the ministry which the Laudians favoured. His outspoken defence of presbyteral ordering in emergency situations, while it was defensible, threatened the hardening position that episcopal ordination was necessary. If Baxter and the presbyterians were able to read their doctrine of ministry into the Ordinal so that the Ordinal could signify a different ministry than that the Laudians intended the Ordinal to confer, then the Ordinal needed revision in an explicit Laudian direction. In this the episcopal party and the government closed ranks. The revision of the 1662 Ordinal was as much political as it was doctrinal. In so far as it was doctrinal it reflected the teaching of the Bishop of Durham, John Cosin.

John Cosin

John Cosin had long been interested in liturgical matters including the ordination rites. Because of his interest in the Ordinal he and his chaplain, William Sancroft, were the major figures in the revision of the Ordinal in 1662. Cosin was one of the episcopal representatives at the Savoy conference. [72] The political ambience of the settlement precluded acceptance of Cosin's Notes and Corrections for Prayer Book revision; the preference was for a return to the 1604 (Jacobean) Prayer Book. [73] However Cosin and Matthew Wren succeeded in winning approval for several changes in the Communion Service in the direction of Cranmer's first liturgy in 1549. In the 1661 Convocation Cosin was secretary at the preliminary meetings concerning liturgical revision. Later he was a member of the

---

[72] James Parker, *An Introduction to the History of the Secessive Revisions of the Book of Common Prayer,* Oxford, 1877, pp. lxxix-lxxx.

[73] G.J. Cuming 'The Making of the Prayer Book of 1662', in The Archbishop of Canterbury *et al, The English Prayer Book,* 1549-1662, London, 1963, p. 99.

J

revision committee; most changes that won acceptance were in his handwriting or that of Sancroft. [74] The revision of the Ordinal reflected the doctrine of Cosin.

Cosin's doctrine of the episcopacy diverged from that of the presbyterians and from moderate non-conformists such as Baxter. His study of the Fathers and the early liturgies had convinced him that in the Christian priesthood bishops succeeded the apostles, priests the seventy disciples, and deacons the Jewish levites. Therefore there were three separate and distinct grades in the hierarchy.

> 'It is the full consent of revered antiquity to distinguish the ministers of the Gospel into the degrees answerable to the triple order under the Law, as servants to the same Trinity, the God both of Law and Gospel. There are bishops, successors to the apostles, answerable to the High Priest, presbyters succeeding the seventy disciples, answerable to the priests, and deacons, instituted by the apostles, answerable to the levites.' [75]

Cosin's teaching differed from that of the presbyterians and Roman Catholics. He opposed private masses; [76] against protestants who permitted deacons to preside at the eucharist he declared that only priests and bishops could celebrate mass. Early in his career Cosin took issue with those who extended the functions of deacons.

> 'Doth he take upon him being but a deacon only, and not yet admitted into the sacred order of priesthood, to consecrate the holy Sacrament of the Eucharist, or to pronounce the absolution of sins, either in the preparation to matins, and evensong, or in the administration of the Lord's Supper, or in the visitation of the sick, after confession?' [77]

---

[74] F.S. Brightman, *The English Rite,* 2 Vols. London, 1921, Vol. I, p. ccx.
[75] 'A Sermon at the Consecration of Dr Francis White, Bishop of Carlisle', in *Works of John Cosin,* Vol. I, p. 99.
[76] Notes and Collections in a learned Book of Common Prayer, 1619, *Ibid.,* Vol. V, p. 98.
[77] Articles to be Inquired of by the Church Wardens and Swornmen of Every Parish Within the Archdeanery of East Riding, 1627, *Ibid.,* Vol. II, p. 9.

In his *Book of Devotions* Cosin stressed the gradation in the ministry. Priests were superior to deacons although both grades were licensed to preach. [78] Prelates were superior to priests. The laity were to obey the clergy. 'To submit ourselves daily and reverently to them that are our spiritual guides and fathers, the Prelates and Priests of God's Church.' [79]

Cosin argued that the preaching office was exaggerated by the Puritans. The preaching office of bishops was more comprehensive than that of priests; for this reason bishops licensed other preachers. [80] As successors of the apostles bishops were sent by Christ; priests functioned as their substitutes, serving under the 'pastor' of a diocese.

> 'Christ was sent to preach the gospel to the poor; and of the same errand are His apostles and Bishops sent, "Go ye and teach all nations". The priests' office not so large, who preach too, but yet under the bishop's licence only; they then to be the great pastor of the diocese and we but as servants and substitutes under them, to preach by their commission and not by our own. [81]

Cosin did not endorse the theory of parity as voiced by Baxter and the presbyterians. The biblical term 'pastor' was reserved to bishops, the governors of a diocese. 'Grant that thy Church, being always preserved from false apostles, may be ordered and guided by faithful and true pastors.' [82] The bishop's role as pastor and leader, enjoying the power to appoint ministers, is clear from the ordination prayer in the *Devotions*. 'Guide and govern the minds of thy servants, the Bishops and pastors of thy flock, that they may lay hands suddenly on no man, but faithfully and wisely make choice of fit persons to serve in the Sacred Ministry of thy Church.' [83]

---

[78] The Preface Touching Prayer, in *A Collection of Private Devotions*, London, 1681; n.p.

[79] The Duties of the Fifth Commandment, *Ibid.*, n.p.

[80] Articles to be Inquired, *Works*, Vol. II, p. 7.

[81] Sermon at the Consecration of Dr White, *Ibid.*, Vol. I, p. 95.

[82] The Collect for St Matthew's Day, *A Collection of Devotions*, p. 251; cf. p. 253.

[83] For the Ordination of Priests and Deacons, *Ibid.*, p. 312.

The subordinate role of priests was further emphasized in
the titles attributed to them — minister, parson, vicar and curate.
'Is the mansion — house of your parson, vicar or minister ...
sufficiently repaired? ... Does your parson, vicar or minister in
his teaching, doing, living make himself an example unto others
of godliness?' [84] The parson, vicar or minister received his licence
to preach from a university or 'by the bishop.' [85]

Bishops were the 'height' and 'princes' of the clergy, [86]
successors of the apostles in place and function, independent of
lower ministers in the exercise of jurisdiction. Nor were they
like Roman Catholic prelates 'slaves for the Roman See'. [87]
Against Roman repudiation of Anglican ministry Cosin argued
that the Church of England preserved the apostolic succession.
Referring to the Nag's Head Tale and other canards about
Anglican succession Cosin wrote,

> 'Let them stand and devise such mischievous fables of
> a Church which deserves them not; which even held firm
> (and we are able to make it good) in a continued line of
> succession from former known bishops, and from this
> very mission of the apostles.' [88]

Bishops enjoyed a power of the keys over and above that of
priests. They sent priests and deacons as Christ sent the
apostles (Mt 28.20). They possessed the supreme power to
forgive and retain sins. Through them Christ continued the
power of orders in his church. They also had the power to
suspend the exercise of this power when it was abused. The
bishop's power of jurisdiction was singular to them. [89]

Therefore Cosin approved of the diocesan system and found
it scriptural. Bishops were 'pastors' of a diocese. Presbyters were
their surrogates who extended their preaching to the local
congregations. The presbyterate was not diminished by the

---

[84] Articles to be Inquired, *Works*, Vol. II, pp. 5-6.
[85] *Ibid.*, p. 7.
[86] Sermon at the Consecration of Dr White, *Works*, Vol. I, pp. 100-101.
[87] The History of Popish Transubstantiation, *Works*, Vol. IV, p. 229.
[88] Sermon at the Consecration of Dr White, *Works*, Vol. I, p. 93.
[89] *Ibid.*, pp. 88-100.

bishop's superior power; for this was the order established by Christ. Bishops were answerable to Christ alone for stewardship.

Cosin contradicted the arguments of Baxter and the presbyterians that presbyters could ordain. Arguing from his own understanding of church history Cosin claimed that no priest had ever conferred orders. 'Neither is there any one example to be found in all the stories of the Church of any holy orders that were ever given but by a bishop.... It is none of theirs, they were not sent for this purpose.' [90]

The high doctrine of episcopacy held by Cosin and the Laudians prevailed in the proceedings for revision of the Ordinal. The changes incorporated in the rite reflect Cosin's teaching and counter the teaching of Richard Baxter.

Changes in the Ordinal

The doctrinal changes in the 1662 Ordinal were few but significant. It is important to notice that the points at issue were not sacrifice and the priest's role at the eucharist but the role of episcopacy — the distinction of grades in the ministry. The presbyterians tended to blur the distinction and to favour a presbyteral or synodal form of government, the parity of ministers and presbyteral ordering. Where episcopacy was admitted, as it was by Baxter, Usher, Reynolds and other moderate nonconformists, it was not the exalted and differentiated episcopacy championed by the Laudians.

In 1662 the title of the Ordinal was slightly altered so as to read, 'The form and manner of making, *ordaining* and consecrating bishops, priests and deacons.' [91] Priests and deacons were

---

[90] *Ibid.*, p. 99.

[91] 'The Form and Manner of Making, Ordaining and Consecrating Bishops, Priests, and Deacons According to the Order of the Church of England', in *The Book of Common Prayer and Administration of the Sacraments and of Other Rites and Ceremonies of the Church According to the Use of the Church of England*, London, 1680, n.p. All references to the 1662 Ordinal are taken from this edition, printed by His Majesty's printer, J. Bull, Newcomb and Hills.

ordained; bishops were consecrated. There was added, 'according to the order of the Church of England', the Church of England was a part of the universal church in which the apostolic ministry was continued.

The preface stipulated that a person was a legitimate minister if he was ordered 'by public prayer, with imposition of hands, approved and admitted thereunto *by lawful authority*', the last three words being inserted to counter irregular ordinations such as had occurred during the interregnum. A similar change indicated that presbyteral ordering was not sufficient for continuance of the apostolic ministry. The historical context which occasioned the restoration Ordinal may be seen when the preface is compared with that of 1552.

1552	1662
'And therefore, to the intent these orders should be continued, and reverently used, and esteemed, in this Church of England; it is requisite, that no man (not being at this present Bishop, Priest, nor Deacon) shall execute any of them, except he be called, tried, examined and admitted, according to the form hereafter following.'	'And therefore to the intent that these orders may be continued and reverently used and esteemed in the Church of England, no man shall be accounted or taken to be a lawful Bishop, Priest or Deacon in the Church of England, or suffered to execute any of the said functions, except he be called, tried, examined and admitted thereunto according to the form hereafter following, or hath had formerly episcopal consecration or ordination.'

Verbal changes in the opening rubric for ordination of deacons explicitate the distinctions in the hierarchy. 'Minister', 'orders' and 'vocation' give way to terms which clearly designate the diaconate.

1552	1662
'When the day appointed by the Bishop is come,	'When the day appointed by the Bishop is come,

there shall be an exhortation, declaring the duty and
office of such as come to
be admitted Ministers, how
necessary such Orders are
in the Church of Christ,
and also, how the people
ought to esteem them in
their vocation.'

after Morning Prayer is
ended, there shall be a
Sermon or Exhortation,
declaring the duty and
office of such as come to
be admitted deacons; how
necessary that order is in
the Church of Christ; and
also how the people ought
to esteem them in their
office.'

A second rubric permitted vestments; deacons were to be
'decently clad'. Whereas in 1552 they were 'admitted' they are
now explicitly 'to be admitted Deacons', they must be worthy
of admission 'to that office'.

We have observed that according to John Cosin 'pastor'
meant bishop; this title, which is used by the author of the
epistle to the Ephesians, is not a generic title for ministers. The
1662 Ordinal reflected Cosin's teaching when, in the litany, it
explicitated the distinction in the three grades of the hierarchy.

1552

1662

'That it may please thee,
to illuminate all Bishops,
Pastors, and ministers of
the Church, with true
knowledge, and under-
standing of thy word, and
that both by their preaching and living they may
set it forth, and show it
accordingly.'

'That it may please thee
to illuminate all Bishops,
Priests, and Deacons, with
true knowledge and under-
standing of Thy Word,
and that both by their
preaching and living they
may set it forth and show
it accordingly.'

In a further clarification of grades the 'office now to be
committed' was changed to read 'the order of deacons or priests'.

The word 'congregation' was used sparingly in the 1662
Ordinal and was usually omitted. The following comparison with
1552 illustrates both the emphasis on distinction in the hierarchy
and the preference for words other than congregation.

1552	1662
'It pertains to the office of a Deacon . . . to read holy scripture and Homilies in the congregation, and to instruct the youth in the Catechism, to Baptize. . .'	'It pertains to the Office of a Deacon . . . to read holy Scriptures and homilies in the Church; and to instruct the youth in the Catechism; in the absence of the priest to baptize infants. . .'

The form of ordering priests likewise distinguished clearly between the different grades. The opening rubric concerns 'such as come to be admitted priests' and how necessary 'that order' is in the church. There is a special collect for 'these thy servants now called to the office of Priesthood', that they may succeed in 'this office'. The epistle selected is now from the fourth chapter of Ephesians which refers to the different charisms in the church.

An omission with more than verbal implications was the deletion of 'pastors' from the exhortation of candidates for the priesthood. The change reflected Cosin's insistence that in the New Testament pastor meant bishop. Henceforth the oft-quoted passage in the exhortation read, 'to be messengers, watchmen and stewards of the Lord'. Bishops alone were pastors.

There were other changes in the exhortation. Candidates were to give themselves wholly to this 'office' instead of 'vocation'. They were to be patterns for 'the people' instead of 'congregation' and were examined not in the name of the 'congregation' but of 'God and his church'. They are admitted to the 'order' as well as 'ministry' of priesthood.

The most important change in the ordination rite for priests was, of course, in the 'essential form', the part of the rite by which, with the imposition of hands, priesthood was commonly believed to be conveyed. The form was modified to signify the order (of priesthood) being conveyed. The specific reference to this order, within the context of the 1662 revision, did not refer explicitly to sacrifice. The two forms are compared below.

1552	1662
'Receive the holy ghost: whose sins thou doest forgive, they are forgiven: and whose sins thou doest retain, they are retained: and be thou a faithful dispensor of the word of God, and of his holy Sacraments. In the name of the father, and of the son, and of the holy ghost.'	'Receive the holy ghost for the Office and work of a priest in the church of God now committed unto thee by the imposition of our hands. Whose sins thou dost forgive they are forgiven; and whose sins thou dost retain they are retained. And be thou a faithful dispensor of the word of God, and of his holy sacraments; in the name of the Father, and of the Son, and of the Holy Ghost.'

Within the same addition to the form is an important reference to the bishop's power to ordain. This further signified the distinction of orders in the ministry.

At the transmission of the bible the priest is given power to preach when he is 'lawfully' appointed. Finally, in the concluding rubric there is provision for occasions when the diaconate and the priesthood are given on the same day. The purpose of the rubric is to make clear that the orders are distinct, that some men are admitted to one order, other men to another. Each group is to be presented separately, first the deacons, then the priests. There are different collects, both of which are to be used. The deacons are to be ordered after the epistle, the priests after the gospel.

In the form for the episcopate there is a special collect which compares bishops or 'pastors' to the apostles. Bishops are to preach and 'daily administer the discipline' of the church. Paul's address to the elders at Ephesus is transferred from the rite for priests. This signifies the bishop's succession to the apostolic office of leadership of the entire church including the presbyterate. Two new gospels signify the bishop's succession to the office of the apostles — John 20.19; and Matthew 28.20. A rubric states that the bishop is to be vested 'with his rochet'.

In 1662 the bishop is promoted not 'to the glory of thy name and profit of thy congregation', but for 'the edifying and well governing of thy church'.

The bishop is reminded of his responsibility to ordain sufficient ministers by an addition to the Examination: 'Will you be faithful in ordaining, sending, or laying hands upon others?'

As in the preceding rite for priesthood the most important change was in the essential form. Once again the order conveyed is explicitly mentioned and, once again, the bishop's power to ordain is further signified by the references to 'our' hands.

1552	1662
'Take the holy ghost, and remember that thou stir up the grace of God, which is in thee, by imposition of hands: for God hath not given us the spirit of fear, but of power, and love, and of soberness.'	'Receive the holy Ghost for the Office and work of a Bishop in the Church of God, now committed unto thee by the imposition of our hands. In the Name of the Father, and of the Son, and of the holy Ghost. Amen. And remember that thou stir up the grace of God which is given thee by this Imposition of our hands.'

Conclusion

The Elizabethan and Jacobean settlements adopted the Ordinal of 1552. In the 1662 restoration settlement the Ordinal was revised. The changes were relatively few and were not concerned with the 'supper strife' and the priest's power at the eucharist which had concerned Cranmer in the two previous Ordinal revisions. The changes in the Ordinal in 1662 were meant to counter the spectrum of non-conformist opinions which reduced episcopacy and blurred the distinctions within the hierarchy. Although John Cosin and the Laudians, by returning to the primitive church and the writings of the Fathers, had restored in their teaching and unofficial liturgies a sacrificial dimension to the eucharist and, therefore, to the priest's power, this was not reflected in the new Ordinal. What was signified was that bishops, priests, and deacons were distinct orders and that bishops succeeded the apostles in government, discipline and the power to ordain. Subsequent Catholic apologists were correct in asserting that the additions to the forms in the 1662 Ordinal were not meant to signify the priestly power of sacrifice.

CHAPTER VI

Anglican Ministry since 1662

> 'The development of the thinking in our two communions
> regarding the nature of the church and of the ordained
> ministry, as represented in our statement, has, we con-
> sider, put the issues in a new context.'
>
> Anglican/Roman Catholic International Commission

Until the twentieth century ecumenical mergers and liturgical
experimentation the 1662 Ordinal was used in most Anglican
ordinations. But Anglican Orders have not been an unchallenged
possession. While Anglicans and many protestant and orthodox
churches have acknowledged Anglican ministry official Roman
Catholic teaching has withheld full recognition. This in turn has
cast doubt on the full ecclesial reality of Anglicanism.

A major milestone in the story of Anglican ministry subsequent to the Carolingian settlement occurred some two decades
after the Uniformity Act. In 1684 the Holy Office, after an
investigation of Anglican ministry, passed judgment on the
ordination, with the Ordinal, of 'a certain French Calvinist'[1]
who had petitioned that his orders be declared null. The petitioner had been ordained in the Church of England. Later he

---

[1] A substantial part of the Holy Office documents on the French
Calvinist case were published in S. M. Brandi, *La Condanna delle
Ordinazioni Anglicane: Studio Storico-Teologico,* Rome, 1908.

returned to France, became a Roman Catholic, and sought permission to marry. His case reached the tribunal of the Holy Office. There were two decisive questions involved: did he, because of his ordination in the Church of England, suffer from the diriment impediment of orders? or was he invalidly ordained and therefore free to marry? The decision was in the negative to the first question, in the affirmative to the second. But first the Holy Office undertook an extensive study of Anglican ministry, including the consultation of theologians in northern Europe. The Congregation concluded that Anglican Orders, especially if conveyed by Anglican bishops, were to be considered as null. The petitioner was therefore free of the diriment impediment of Orders. This decision, involving an otherwise unknown convert, set a precedent for Roman practice concerning Ordinal ministers; for the decision appealed to the practice of the church of reordaining convert Anglican clergymen absolutely as well as to defects of form and intention. [2]

In 1704 the Holy Office again passed judgment, this time concerning a mobile cleric named John Clement Gordon who had been promoted to the bishopric of Galloway under James II. Gordon had been ordained in Scotland in 1668 and consecrated 7 September 1688. Shortly thereafter he abandoned his untimely bishopric and fled to France, episcopacy being abolished in Scotland in July 1689.

After a dubious career in France and Ireland in the Jacobite entourage Gordon moved into the Roman Catholic Church in 1703. Pope Clement XI wished to appoint him to the sinecure post of Abbot of St Clement's but the benefice required at least minor orders. So arose the question of Gordon's orders — *and* his confirmation. He petitioned that his episcopal orders be declared null, pointing to the practice of the church and claiming the Anglican succession had lapsed. [3] On 17th April, 1703, the Holy Office declared *all* of Gordon's orders null; according to the existing practice, cited in the French Calvinist case, he was

---

[2] For a succinct summary of the French Calvinist case see Hughes, *Absolutely Null and Utterly Void,* pp. 278-280.

[3] A.S. Barnes, *The Popes and the Ordinal,* London, 1898, pp. 134-137.

to be re-ordained absolutely to any orders. Accordingly Gordon, eager for a Roman benefice, was reordained to the necessary minor orders. [4]

In 1885, at the request of Cardinal Manning, the Holy Office conducted an investigation of the Ordinal form; that is, the Congregation investigated the Ordinal, its origin and its history to ascertain whether the formula 'Receive the Holy Ghost' was adequate for the conferral of Catholic priesthood. A decisive *votum* was prepared for the Congregation by the eminent theologian Franzelin. The votum is significant because it illustrates the common teaching of Roman theologians on the eve of *Apostolicae Curae* and is, in fact, strikingly similar to the reasoning of the forthcoming bull. [5] Franzelin rejected some tentative theological suggestions that the orthodox intentions of the Carolines and of later Anglican ordainers were capable of rendering the Ordinal apt for conferral of Orders. He denied that use of the Ordinal within an orthodox community could make the form sufficient. The main question, according to Franzelin, was why and how the Ordinal was changed 'by the first Deformers in the reign of Edward VI'. The historical circumstances show that a heterodox rite was introduced and that the form was deficient; therefore Matthew Parker was invalidly consecrated due to defect of form. Franzelin concluded that Anglican ordinations 'at least until the year 1662' were invalid on two counts; defect of form and lapse of power in the succession. Significantly Franzelin did not pass judgment on the 1662 formula and he believed that lack of power in Anglican ordainers had permanently extinguished the Anglican hierarchy. This latter conviction, as we have seen, is questionable on historical grounds.

Franzelin went on to specify the deficiency in the heterodox form. Its framers deleted 'all that signified the priestly power,

---

[4] For a commendable attempt at reconstruction of Gordon's meandering career, see T.F. Taylor, *A Profest Papist, Bishop John Gordon*, London, 1958.

[5] Franzelin's *votum* was not published in full until 1956 when it was published, with permission, from the copy in the Westminster archives, by Francis Clark, *Anglican Orders and Defect of Intention*, pp. 186-188.

which is the power of consecrating and offering the sacrifice of the New Testament'. To delete signification of sacrificial power is to render the form incapable of conferring priestly power.

Catholic theologians and historians, however, continued to question the Roman practice of treating Anglican Orders as null. The Pope decided to settle the controversy 'forever'. [6] Once again a study of Anglican ministry was conducted. The Pope weighed the reports of his commissions and, on 13th September, 1896, issued *Apostolicae Curae* which concluded 'that Ordinations carried out according to the Anglican rite have been and are absolutely null and utterly void.' [7]

In this bull the Pope argued that the words 'Receive the Holy Ghost' did not in themselves signify priesthood. Nor did other parts of the Ordinal add the necessary signification because 'these prayers have been deliberately stripped of everything which in the Catholic rite clearly sets forth the dignity and functions of the priesthood'. The form of the Ordinal, therefore, neither *in se* nor *ex adjunctis* was capable of conveying priestly power. The Pope took account of the addition of 1662: 'for the office and work of a priest [bishop]'. This addition demonstrated that even Anglicans realized that the essential form of the Edwardine Ordinal was defective. Even if (*si forte quidem*) this addition could have lent the form a legitimate signification (*legitimam significationem apponere formae posset*) it was added too late, for the hierarchy had died out and with it the power to ordain.

To the defect in form the Pope briefly added a defect in intention. The defective intention of the consecrators of Matthew Parker in 1559 was clear from their repudiation of the Catholic rite and substitution of a heterodox rite with the purpose of repudiating what the church does and what belongs to the nature of the sacrament. The Pope concluded his arguments for nullity by appealing to the practice of the church.

---

[6] Hughes, *Absolutely Null and Utterly Void*, pp. 28-187.
[7] The text may be found in AAS, Vol. 29, (1896-7), pp. 198-201, and *Anglican Orders* (English), London, 1957.

'Adhering entirely to the decrees of the Pontiffs Our Predecessors on this subject, and fully ratifying and renewing
them by Our own initiatives and with certain knowledge,
We pronounce and declare that ordinations performed
according to the Anglican rite have been and are absolutely
null and utterly void.'

Apostolicae Curae is the most solemn decision ever made by
Rome on the subject of Anglican ordinations. The decision
for non-recognition remains the official position of the Catholic
magisterium. Since it involves the very reality of a sacrament
central to the church the decision is based on the principle
of tutiorism. However despite the hyperbolic language used
by the Pope *Apostolicae Curae* has not been presented nor
received as infallible. It is a solemn decision in continuity
with previous magisterial decrees which must stand unless and
until new data, a new context, and new circumstances make a
variant decision compelling. Within the historical and juridical
context and the defensive theology of priesthood of the post-
Tridentine schools the Pope had asked the customary questions
about Anglican ministry and found it wanting.

The Roman Catholic Church has not been the only church
troubled by the problem of Anglican ministry. In July 1920,
the Orthodox Ecumenical Patriarch urged Orthodoxy to
acknowledge the validity of Anglican Orders. In 1930 the Holy
Synod of Alexandria revised previous hesitancy by pronouncing
that 'if priests, ordained by Anglican bishops, accede to Orthodoxy, they should not be re-ordained.'[8] In 1936, after the
Patriarch of Constantinople had announced his recognition of
validity, the Rumanian Orthodox Church adopted the following
recommendation of a special commission whose conclusion was
more positive than that of the commissions of Leo XIII: 'The
Rumanian Orthodox Commission unanimously recommends the
Holy Synod to recognize the validity of Anglican Orders'.[9] Also
in 1936 the Mar Thoma Syrian Church declared that for its

---

[8] Letter from the Patriarch of Alexandria to the Archbishop of Canterbury, 25 December, 1930, in *Documents of Christian Unity,
Third Series, 1930-1948*, G.K.A. Bell, ed., London, 1948, p. 38.
[9] Resolution of the Holy Synod of the Rumanian Orthodox Church,
20 March, 1936, *Ibid.*, p. 49.

own church and the church of India, Burma and Ceylon, 'there is no ban in respect of the orders, doctrine and worship of either church to the formal establishment of the measure of intercommunion between them which is known as occasional intercommunion'. [10]

Similar events took place in the West. In 1931 the Old Catholic Archbishop of Utrecht informed the Archbishop of Canterbury that 'the Synod assembled in Vienna on September 7, 1931, of the Old Catholic bishops united in the union of Utrecht, on the basis of the recognition of the validity of Anglican ordinations, agrees to intercommunion with the Anglican communion'. [11] In 1946 the American Polish National Catholic Church which was in communion with the See of Utrecht entered into communion with the Episcopal Church of the United States. A joint commission stated in 1947, 'the relationship between the churches, it was agreed, is one of *inter*communion, that is, sacramental communion between two autonomous churches'. [12] The development was hesitant, and not without reversals, but churches of the Catholic tradition as well as protestant churches continued, in the age of ecumenism, to recognize Anglican ministry.

The context was clearly changing. Henceforth bishops whose orders Rome acknowledged increasingly took part in Anglican ordinations. Old Catholics, for example, began to participate in Anglican consecrations in 1922. National Polish Catholic bishops did likewise. Whatever might be said about the signification of the Anglican Ordinal, [13] it could not be said that Anglican ordainers lacked the power to confer orders. [14]

---

[10] The Assembly of the Mar Thoma Syrian Church, Resolution Adopted at its Session of May 5 and 6, 1936, *Ibid.,* p. 58.

[11] Letter from the Archbishop of Utrecht to the Archbishop of Canterbury, September, 1931, *Ibid.,* p. 61.

[12] The Polish National Catholic Church and the Protestant Episcopal Church in the United States of America: Resolution of the Committee on Intercommunion, 27 June, 1947, *Ibid.,* p. 13.

[13] Clark, *Anglican Orders and Defect of Intention,* pp. 192-195.

[14] There is also the interesting development wherein Anglicans may use other *rites* for their ordinations. Cf. Anglican/Methodist Unity Commission, *Anglican/Methodist Unity, I — The Ordinal,* London, 1968.

Moreover, as early as 1896 the Roman magisterium had publically acknowledged developments in Anglican eucharistic *faith*. Although he framed the admission in the negative and polemical context of *Apostolicae Curae* Leo XIII admitted some rapprochment in Anglican and Roman Catholic doctrine. 'It was in vain that in the time of Charles I, some attempted to make room for some part of sacrifice and priesthood ... equally vain is the contention of a fairly small and recently formed section of Anglicans that the rite can be made to bear a sound and orthodox sense.' [15]

Again at Vatican II the Catholic teaching office adverted to Anglican ministry. In its Decree on Ecumenism the Council singled out the Anglican Communion for its preservation of certain Catholic elements, among which is the historic episcopate. [16] 'Among these [ecclesial communities of the West] in which some Catholic traditions and institutions continue to exist the Anglican Communion occupies a special place.' [17] This of course was no recognition of the 'validity' of Anglican Orders. For in its general principles for intercommunion the Decree mentions only Orthodoxy as sharing true priesthood and eucharist.

> 'Although these Churches are separated from us, they possess true sacraments, above all — by apostolic succession — the priesthood and the Eucharist, whereby they are still joined to us in a very close relationship. Therefore, given suitable circumstances and the approval of Church authority, some worship in common is not merely possible but is recommended.' [18]

The Anglican Communion, despite its 'special place' was included among the separated communities of the West when the Council said, 'we believe that especially because of the lack of the sacra-

[15] *AAS*, Vol. 29, p. 200.
[16] Johannes Feiner, 'Commentary on the Decree' in *Commentary on the Documents of Vatican II,* Herbert Vorgrimler, ed., 4 Vols., London, 1968, II, p. 128.
[17] Decree on Ecumenism, in *The Documents of Vatican II,* Walter Abbott, ed., London, 1966, p 356.
[18] *Ibid.,* p. 359.

ment of orders they have not preserved the genuine and total reality of the Eucharistic mystery'. [19] The Council reiterated the traditional Catholic principle that eucharistic sharing must signify integral communion. Only in exceptional and individual cases may (non-Orthodox) separated Christians, including Anglicans, share the Catholic eucharist.

> 'As for common worship, however, it may not be regarded as a means to be used indiscriminately for the restoration of unity among Christians. Such worship depends chiefly on two principles: it should signify the unity of the Church; it should provide a sharing in the means of grace. The fact that it should signify unity generally rules out common worship. Yet the gaining of a needed grace sometimes commends it.' [20]

After the Council the Secretariat for Unity repeated and explained the Catholic discipline; first in its Directory for implementation of the Decree on Ecumenism, [21] again in January 1970, [22] and again, in response to questions raised by ecumenists, theologians and other Christians, including those in mixed marriages, in June 1972. [23] This latter document, signed by Cardinal Willebrands and Jerome Hamer and approved by Pope Paul VI, is a nuanced exposition of the prevailing Catholic discipline. Nor did the Secretariat alter its basic position in 1973.

The Secretariat explained that the Eucharist signifies integral faith and ecclesial communion: it contains the foundation of the being and unity of the church, the Body and Blood of Christ given to the church. Communal eucharistic sharing with separated Christians, including Anglicans, is inappropriate; for the eucharist of its nature comprehends three elements,

> '— the ministerial power which Christ gave to his apostles and to their successors, the bishops along with the priests,

---

[19] *Ibid.*, p. 364.
[20] *Ibid.*, p. 352.
[21] *Ecumenical Directory I*, nn. 44, 55.
[22] SPCU Information Service, 1970/71, pp. 21-23.
[23] Instructions Concerning Cases When Other Christians May be Admitted to Eucharistic Communion in the Catholic Church, 1 June, 1972, in *The Clergy Review*, August, 1973, pp. 633-639.

to make effective sacramentally his own priestly act — that
act by which once and forever he offered himself to the
Father in the Holy Spirit, and gave himself to his faithful
that they might be one in him;

— the unity of the ministry, which is to be exercised in
the name of Christ, Head of the Church, and hence in
the hierarchical communion of ministers;

— the faith of the Church, which is expressed in the
eucharistic action itself: the faith by which she responds
to Christ's gift in its true meaning.

The sacrament of the Eucharist, understood in its
entirety with these three elements, signifies an existing unity
brought about by Him, the unity of the visible Church of
Christ which cannot be lost.' [24]

Clearly the major obstacle to intercommunion is the 'defectum'
in the Sacrament of Orders.

'The *Directorium Oecumenicum* gives different directions
for the admission to holy communion of separated Eastern
Christians, and of others. The reason is that the Eastern
Churches, though separated from us, have true sacraments,
above all, because of the apostolic succession, the priesthood and the Eucharist, which unite them to us by close
ties, so that the risk of obscuring the relation between
eucharistic communion and ecclesial communion is somewhat reduced.' [25]

However, the Decree on Ecumenism mandated dialogue on
ministry and eucharist. Since the Council this mandate has been
implemented with results that none had foreseen in the early
sixties. [26] Repeatedly Anglican/Roman Catholic Commissions,
many of them under joint official auspices, have reported basic
convergence on eucharistic faith. The conclusions reached by
competent and representative commissions have been virtually
the same as that reached by the official American Anglican/
Roman Catholic commission in 1967. 'Whatever doctrinal dis-

---

[24] *Ibid.*, p. 634.
[25] *Ibid.*, p. 638.
[26] Echlin, *The Anglican Eucharist in Ecumenical Perspective*, pp. 238-
240.

agreements may remain between our churches, the understanding of the sacrificial nature of the eucharist is not among them.' [27]

In March 1966, at the conclusion of their unprecedented meeting, the Archbishop of Canterbury and Pope Paul VI announced in a *Common Declaration* their intention to sponsor 'serious' dialogue between their churches. A joint preparatory commission was promptly established which, at Malta in 1967, recommended a 'permanent' commission with the ultimate goal organic unity. The resultant international commission determined, at Venice in 1970, to concentrate its efforts on three historically divisive issues — eucharist, ministry, authority. At Windsor, in September 1971, the commission presented a remarkable 'Agreed Statement' on the eucharist.

The statement on the eucharist revealed the methodology the commission was to follow — 1) to reach 'substantial' or 'basic' agreement; 2) on the principal doctrines which have previously divided the two churches and concerning which basic agreement is necessary for organic reunion; 3) which agreement is 'consonant with biblical teaching and with the tradition of our common inheritance'; and 4) to formulate this agreement for discussion and discernment by both churches.

Accordingly in 1971 the commission reported 'substantial agreement' on the eucharist including the previously divisive doctrines of eucharistic sacrifice and real presence. The commission expressed its agreement on sacrifice by having recourse to the biblical concept of memorial. 'The notion of *memorial* as understood in the passover celebration at the time of Christ — i.e. the making effective in the present of an event in the past — has opened the way to a clearer understanding of the relationship between Christ's sacrifice and the eucharist.' [28] The doctrine of the presence was expressed in clear language which expresses the mystery just as, in other epochs, language such

---

[27] Report of the fourth meeting of the joint commission on Anglican-Roman Catholic Relations in the United States of America, Milwaukee, Wisconsin, May 4-6, 1967, in *The Journal of the General Convention* (Episcopal Church), 1967.

[28] Agreed Statement on the Eucharist, September, 1971, in *Modern Eucharistic Agreement*, London, 1973, p. 27.

as transubstantiation and transformation expressed it. Basing
their affirmation on scripture and the common inheritance the
commission did not attempt to explain the 'how' of the mystery.
'Communion with Christ in the eucharist presupposes His true
presence, effectually signified by the bread and wine which, in
this mystery, become His body and blood.' [29] The commission
concluded its brief statement with the hope that 'in view of the
agreement which we have reached on eucharistic faith, this
doctrine will no longer constitute an obstacle to the unity we
seek'. [30]

In September 1973, the Anglican/Roman Catholic International Commission reached 'basic agreement' on the doctrine
of ministry. [31] The agreed statement discussed the ministry not
in isolation but within the church and the pluriform ministries
of all Christians. The priest is seen as leader and focus of unity,
with the essential function of supervision. The priesthood of the
ordained ministry differs in quality from the royal priesthood
which it leads and serves. The commission prepared the ground-
work for eventual recognition of Anglican ministry by acknowl-
edging the pluralism in the primitive ministry and the gradual
development of the mono-episcopate.

The priest's role at the eucharist is representative of his role
as leader and unifier. Because he represents the one and only
high priest at the memorial of Christ's sacrifice both Anglican
and Roman Catholic traditions recognize their ministers as
priests. In the Agreed Statement of 1973 there is no undue
emphasis on the priest's role at the eucharist and certainly no
trace either of the popular theology against which the reformers
reacted or of their over-reaction against Catholic priesthood.

The commission used different data than had its predecessors of both traditions, namely the findings of modern exegesis;

---

[29] *Ibid.*, p. 28. In a footnote the Commission explained that in
(modern?) Catholic theology the use of 'transubstantiation' is meant
to affirm the reality of the change and new presence but not to
explain the 'how'.

[30] *Ibid.*, p. 29.

[31] *Ministry and Ordination*: A Statement on the Doctrine of the
Ministry Agreed By the Anglican/Roman Catholic International
Commission, Canterbury, 1973, p. 1.

it worked with a different world-view and, therefore, with a different concept of sacrament; it enjoyed new insights and, above all, it asked different questions of the Christian and Anglican ministry than had been asked by Roman authorities from the time of Reginald Pole to the decrees of the Unity Secretariat.

The commission made no direct recommendation about the *recognition* of Anglican ministry. But the Canterbury Statement leaves no doubt that, having announced agreement on eucharist and ministry and formulated that agreement for discernment by both churches, the commission expects the Church of Rome, under the guidance of the Spirit, to ascertain why and how, in the near future, Anglican Orders may be acknowledged as 'valid' by Rome.

> 'We are fully aware of the issues raised by the judgment of the Roman Catholic Church on Anglican Orders. The development of the thinking in our two commissions regarding the nature of the church and of the ordained ministry, as represented in our Statement, has, we consider, put these issues in a new context. Agreement on the nature of ministry is prior to the consideration of the mutual recognition of ministries.' [32]

Towards Recognition

In the remainder of these pages I propose to discuss briefly a contemporary approach to Anglican Orders which asks questions that were not put forward in the nineteenth century and, thereafter, to suggest some methodological guidelines for a contemporary appropriation of *Apostolicae Curae*. For this bull, despite the development at Vatican II to which we have briefly referred, remains official Roman teaching. It is not infidelity to our predecessors to acknowledge that we are asking different questions about the ministry than were asked in the nineteenth century and that our questions may result in different decisions. I do not believe that *Apostolicae Curae*, which will always be part of our '*memoria Christi*', should be bypassed. Nor do I believe that the arguments and decision of *Apostolicae Curae*

---

[32] *Ibid.*, p. 8.

should be repeated uncritically in a different historical context
than that of 1896. What concerns us today is an honest appropriation of *Apostolicae Curae* for a different historical context so
that this document may remain a received part of our heritage
as we join in full communion with our Anglican brothers.

We realize today that there was a pluralism of mutually
recognized ministries in the early Church which coexisted in
full communion. [33] Since the sixteenth century there has been
a resurgence of pluralism which has not always been mutually
recognized. We are asking whether Churches with varied ordering who substantially agree on the doctrines of eucharist and
presbyterate can recognize each other's ministries. We are asking
whether, since the fragmentation of the sixteenth century, there
has not been a resurgence of eucharistic convergence. [34] We are
asking whether Rome, whose theologians profess substantial
agreement with Anglican doctrine of eucharist and priesthood,
can recognize Anglican priesthood as 'valid' against the background of the precedent for a pluralism of ministries in the
primitive church. We are asking if the present state of division
is not at least as much of an emergency situation as was the

---

[33] Among the authors sympathetic to an approach I would call pluralist are Hans Küng, *Structures of the Church*, London, 1964, pp.
133-156, and *The Church*, New York, 1967, pp. 363f; George
Tavard, 'The Function of the Minister in the Eucharist: An Ecumenical Approach', in *The Journal of Ecumenical Studies*, Vol. IV
(1967), pp. 629-649; 'Roman Catholic Theology and Recognition
of Ministry', *Ibid.*, Vol. VI (1969), pp. 623-628; 'Anglican Orders —
Again', *One in Christ*, Vol. VII (1971), pp. 46-54; Maurice Villain,
'Can There Be Apostolic Succession Outside the Chain of Imposi-
tion of Hands?', *Concilium*, Vol. XXXIV (1968), pp. 87-104;
Harry J. McSorley, 'Trent and the Question: Can Protestant
Ministers Confect the Eucharist', *Worship*, Vol. 43, No. 10, pp. 574-
589; 'The Competent Minister of the Eucharist in Ecumenical
Perspective', *One in Christ*, Vol. V, 1969, pp. 405-423; Myles
Bourke, 'Reflections on Church Order in the New Testament', *The
Catholic Biblical Quarterly*, Vol. XXX (1968), pp. 493-511; Raymond
E. Brown, *'Priest and Bishop'*, N.Y., 1970, pp. 82-86; Kilian
McDonnell, 'Ways of Validating Ministry', in *The Journal of
Ecumenical Studies*, 7, 1970, pp. 244-254; C.K. Barrett, *The Signs
of an Apostle*, London, 1970.

[34] Edward P. Echlin, *The Anglican Eucharist in Ecumenical Perspective*, pp. 237-241.

state of development towards historic episcopate in the early church.

As we look to the primordial ministry we observe that Christ imparted *order* to his church. What made a Christian minister was not birth (like the high priests) or learning (like the scribes) but a vocation, mission, and endowment with the grace of God (Jn 21.15-17). Christ did not ordain bishops nor explicitly enjoin the episcopate nor a succession of consecrating bishops. [35] The church, under the guidance of the Spirit and the leadership of the apostles, structured itself gradually; and different forms coexisted in full communion, a pluralism of mutually recognized ministries.

The early Pauline communities were, it seems, very loosely structured at the local level. [36] 'God has given the first place to apostles, the second to prophets, the third to teachers; after them miracles, and after them, the gift of healing, helpers, good leaders, those with many languages' (1 Cor. 12.28). At Rome a similar charismatic ministry was widely shared. 'If your gift is prophecy, then use it as your faith suggests; if administration, then use it for administration; if teaching, then use it for teaching' (Rom 12.7). There were at Philippi leaders called by Paul — without any further explanation — *episcopoi* and *diaconoi* (Phil. 1.1) and at Thessalonica there were administrators 'who are working among you and who are above you in the Lord as your teachers' (1 Thess. 5:13; cf. Rom. 12.7). Paul himself exercised strong albeit mobile leadership over his churches. 'You have done well in remembering me so constantly and in passing on the traditions just as I passed them on to you' (1 Cor. 11.2; cf. 7.17). Luke even says that Paul appointed *presbyters* in his churches. 'In each of their churches they [Paul and Barnabas] appointed elders, and with prayer and fasting they commended them to the Lord in whom they had

[35] Raymond E. Brown, *Priest and Bishop*, pp. 47-86; L.S. Greenslade, 'Scripture and Other Doctrinal Norms in Early Theories of the Ministry', in *The Journal of Theological Studies*, Vol. XLIV (1943), pp. 162-177, esp. 162-166.
[36] Myles Bourke, 'Reflections on Church Order in the New Testament', *The Catholic Biblical Quarterly*, pp. 510-511.

come to believe' (Acts 14.23; cf. 20.17). Therefore the argument that the presbyteral system was lacking in the early Pauline communities is from silence and should be used with caution.

Nevertheless, we believe the evidence permits the verdict that the early Pauline churches, under the direction of the apostle, were more loosely structured than some of their sister churches. The supervision of Paul made a loose structure possible. There was therefore a pluralism of ministries especially between the gentile and Jewish Christian churches.

The mother church of Jerusalem structured itself differently than the gentile churches. There were at Jerusalem, in addition to Peter and the twelve, James the Lord's brother and a college of presbyters (Acts 6.1-6; 15). The Jerusalem church was, however, in full communion with the more loosely structured churches under the guidance of Paul (Gal. 2.10; Rom. 15.25-27). Rudolf Schnackenburg observes, 'the original apostles recognized the apostolate of Paul, and Paul joined their ranks as the last witness of Jesus' resurrection, submitted his gospel to them, and maintained connection with Jerusalem' [37]

The Pastoral epistles, whether written by Paul or a descendant, reveal that presbyteral ordering emerged even in the gentile churches. Paul had appointed delegates or 'second grade apostles' to supervise the missionary churches and to appoint colleges of residential presbyters. 'The reason I left you behind in Crete was for you to get everything organized there and appoint elders in every town, in the way I told you' (Tit. 1.5; cf. 1 Tim. 3.1-5). The delegates and their residential colleagues were commissioned to preserve the gospel (2 Tim. 1.13), teach (2.24), and govern (1 Tim. 5.5), but neither the delegates nor the presbyters under their supervision were the monarchical bishops of later decades.

As the original apostles and their delegates passed away residential ordering under one leader soon developed. The author of II John spoke with authority to several churches, but in III John we observe that a local leader, Diotrephes, who

---

[37] Rudolf Schnackenburg, *The Church in the New Testament*, N.Y., 1965, p. 102.

'ranks first' is unwilling to acknowledge John's leadership or to admit his emissaries (cf. III Jn 9-10). Possibly this was the beginning of the mono-episcopate. It seems that late in the first century the authority of mobile and regional 'apostles' was clearly on the wane. [38]

1 Clement (c. 96) reveals that late in the first century there were presbyters even at Corinth. Clement goes beyond the evidence when he states without nuance that the apostles themselves appointed *episcopoi* and deacons and provided for their succession. [39] The way presbyteral ordering at Corinth took place remains open. Presbyters may have been appointed by Paul, a delegate, other presbyters, or by those not themselves ordained; or they may not have been formally ordained at all. The important point is that the presbyters at Corinth were, albeit not without tension, recognized by the community as their ministers *and* as presidents at the eucharist. 'It will undoubtedly be no light offence on our part if we remove from their bishopric men who have been performing its duties with impeccable devotion' (1 Clem. 44; cf. 42).

But a pluralism of mutually recognized ministries was still operative. The Didache testifies to a continuing ministry of prophets and teachers late in the first century. The didachist recommends the appointment of *episcopoi* and deacons who are worthy of the Lord: men who are humble and not eager for money, but sincere and approved; for they carry out the ministry of the prophets and teachers' (Did. 15).

Some pluralism of ministry perdured into the second century. For Ignatius of Antioch the recently developed *triadic* ministry was necessary to the church.

'Likewise let all respect the deacons as Jesus Christ, even as the bishop is also a type of the Father, and the presbyter as the Council of God and the apostles. Without these the name of church is not rightly given (Trall 3.1).'

[38] Brown, *Priest and Bishop*, pp. 74-75.

[39] Greenslade, 'Scripture and Other Doctrinal Norms in Early Theories of the Ministry', *The Journal of Theological Studies*, pp. 162-166.

Yet in his letter to the church at Rome Ignatius makes no
mention of a monarchical bishop and the author of the 'Shepherd
of Hermes' who was familiar with the Roman scene writes of
episcopoi in the plural and seems to refer to a considerably
looser structure than that extolled by Ignatius.

> 'The stones which are square and white and fit into their
> joints are the apostles and bishops and teachers and dea-
> cons who walked according to the magistry of God, and
> served the elect of God in holiness and reverence as bishops
> and teachers and deacons; some of them are fallen asleep
> and some are still alive (Hermes 3.5.1).'

It is clear from these early Christian writings that the triadic
ministry was developing in the second century. But the development was fitful and discontinuous and not without tensions.
Significantly, Jerome wrote two centuries later that presbyters
participated in the ordering of the Alexandrian bishopric well
into the third century. [40] We may conclude that not all *episcopoi-
presbyteroi* are clearly traceable to ordination by an apostle, that
some of them may have been ordained by persons not themselves ordained, that some may not have been formally ordained
at all, that a pluralism of mutually recognized ministries existed
for some time in communities which were in substantial agreement on the doctrines of eucharist and ministry, that a pluralism
of officers presided at the eucharist, that these ministries were
recognized by the churches as 'valid', and that they are still
recognized as 'valid' by the Roman Church today.

A word remains to be said on early eucharistic ministry.
A Christian priesthood, replacing the Jewish one, emerged
explicitly only after the destruction of the Temple and with the
dawning awareness of the eucharist as an unbloody sacrifice and
the ministry as a priesthood. The New Testament does not say
explicitly that the *episcopoi-presbyteroi* presided at the eucharist
(cf. 1 Tim. 3.1-5). Paul never says explicitly that he presided
although he almost certainly included himself when speaking
of 'the cup which we bless' (1 Cor. 10.16); and Luke seems to
portray him as president at Troas (Acts 20.11). Yet it is signi-

---

[40] Jerome, 'Epistle ad Evangelum', PL 22:1192-1195.

ficant that in eighteen months at Corinth Paul seemingly baptized
only two individuals and one household (1 Cor. 1.14-15) —
hardly a record of *cultic* ministry. We may presume the twelve
presided at the eucharst — the 'Do this in commemoration of
me' is addressed to them (Lk. 22.19; but cf. 1 Cor. 11.24).

But the apostles (and later, the presbyters) were not the only
presidents. We have observed in the Didache that prophets and
teachers presided at the liturgy (Didache 15; cf. 10.7) and Luke
has prophets 'liturgizing' (Acts 13.1-2). By the time of Ignatius
of Antioch (c. 107) the bishop was the ordinary president: 'Let
that be considered a valid eucharist which is celebrated by the
bishop or by one whom he appoints' (Smyrn 8.2). There seems
to be no compelling evidence for the traditional theory that all
sacramental powers were given to the twelve, and that they communicated these powers to others who in turn transmitted them
to residential presbyter-bishops. There was in fact a pluralism
of early eucharistic presidency — and these pluralistic ministries
were acknowledged by the churches as 'valid'. Sacramental
powers were communicated by Christ to the church — and the
church distributed these powers. What was always constant was
the recognition by the church of those who functioned as ministers. How these powers were transmitted, how long they endured,
and who exercised them is not certain. What is clear is that a
community recognized these ministers as having received sacramental powers from God and that different communities recognized each other's ministries and eucharists. As Schnackenburg
writes, 'The celebration of the eucharist was from the beginning
the central and common worship of the Christian churches; it
was peculiar to them in commemoration of their Lord and in
fulfilment of his sacred command, and intrinsically bound them
together'. [41]

Since the sixteenth century there has been a resurgence of
pluralism in eucharistic ministries. Today we are asking that if,
as Leo XIII contended, the reformers rejected sacrificial priesthood and severed the Catholic succession, can eucharistic faith
and ministry so revive that we can once again acknowledge a

---

[41] Schnackenburg, *The Church in the New Testament*, p. 18.

diversity of apostolic ministries? In the pluralism that existed in the early church is there a precedent for mutual recognition of ministries and eucharist? In our new historical and theological context can Rome acknowledge Anglican Orders and eucharists as 'valid'? Myles Bourke observes,

> 'The now widespread recognition of the diversity of order in the New Testament Churches has brought many to the belief that there is a possibility for Christian Churches formerly seriously opposed on the questions of order to recognise one another as representing an authentic ordering of the Church; thereby the door to accepting the reality of the sacraments of other Churches, and, in some cases, to serious proposals for corporate reunion has been opened, however cautiously.' [42]

Anglicans and Roman Catholics find their eucharists in the New Testament and in joint statements of eucharistic convergence. [43] Both churches are committed to the continuance of apostolic ministry as it was established by Christ and structured by the church. [44] Anglicans recognize Roman Catholic bishops and priests as well as their own bishops and priests as 'valid' ministers. Even without Roman recognition Anglican Orders are 'valid' within the Anglican Communion. They are acknowledged by Anglicans, as far as human powers are able to discern as apt for recognition as authentic orders. The remaining '*defectum*' in Anglican Orders seems to be the non-recognition of the Roman Catholic Church. Validity therefore means that Orders are considered 'proven' to be apt for recognition; non-validity (in the case at hand) means that Rome maintains they are 'not proven' as apt for recognition. [45] When Rome *does* consider Anglican Orders as 'proven' we submit that this should be

---

[42] Myles Bourke, 'Reflections on Church Order in the New Testament', *The Catholic Biblical Quarterly*, p. 493.

[43] Harry J. McSorley, 'Unprecedented Agreement on the Eucharist', *The Ecumenist*, September-October, 1970, pp. 89-90.

[44] Gregory Dix, *The Question of Anglican Orders*, London, 1956, p. 78.

[45] John Coventry, 'Anglican Orders: Reassessing the Debate', *New Blackfriars*, January, 1971, pp. 38-40; but cf. Portal Mercier, 'Anglican Orders: a New Context', *The Ampleforth Journal*, Spring, 1974, pp. 28-36.

acknowledged in a public act, possibly through a pronouncement by the Pope in union with the episcopal college. Raymond Brown writes,

> 'Recognition by the Church is what is essential for sacred ministry; ordination by the laying on of a bishop's hand is simply the standard way of conferring recognition in episcopally structured Churches, and in the novel instance of Church union an alternative form of recognition could be introduced, namely, a proclamation of the acceptance of validity by the Pope.' [46]

A Reappropriation of 'Apostolicae Curae'

If the response to the new questions asked by the pluralist approach is positive — as I believe it must be — we may still retain *Apostolicae Curae* (with a continuing function) as part of the *'memoria'* of the Church. Piet Fransen writes,

> 'A statement of the Church is *primarily* valid for its contemporaries and has only a secondary, though very important, significance for later generations. In the meantime the situation has changed, the crisis and therefore the question has disappeared, and the language asks for an interpretation. But this 'confessional statement' necessarily still belongs to the public *'memoria'* of the living Church and therefore continues its function though in a very different context and in a different way.' [47]

In conclusion I wish to propose some methodological guidelines for a contemporary interpretation and appropriation of *Apostolicae Curae* which will continue its function 'in a different context and in a different way'.

1. The bull is not infallible teaching. Considering the restricted context and questions of *Apostolicae Curae* I believe the decision of the bull was proper. Nevertheless there have been cogent arguments, including those put forward by the Anglican

---

[46] Brown, *Priest and Bishop*, p 84.
[47] Piet Fransen, 'Unity and Confessional Statements', unpublished paper.

Archbishops contemporary with Leo XIII, that the bull's arguments and decision were wrong. [48] At a minimum Roman Catholics must remain open to the possibility that the bull's teaching, because it is not infallible, could be wrong. And Church authorities must be open to the possibility that in the future they may be required to admit the decision was wrong. Avery Dulles observes,

'In point of fact theologically educated Catholics have always known that the vast majority of the Church's teaching is fallible and therefore subject to error... But if a given doctrine is not infallible it is fallible; in other words it could be wrong. Having once conceded that their teaching could be wrong Church authorities should not be afraid to admit, when the occasion requires, that they have been wrong.' [49]

2. The triumphalist language employed by the bull should not be taken literally. Roman documents have often resorted to evocative language to educe assent from wavering Catholics. Leo XIII was aware that some Catholics, including eminent continental theologians and even a minority of his preparatory commission, were questioning the traditional practice of treating Anglican Orders as null. The Pope wished to put an end to the discussion and thereby induce Anglicans to return to Rome. Triumphant language such as the following should be received as a literary form intended to evoke assent.

'All these matters have been long and carefully considered by Ourselves and by Our Venerable Brethren, the Judges of the Supreme Council, of whom it has pleased Us to call a special meeting upon the "Feria V" the 16th day of July last, upon the solemnity of Our Lady of Mount Carmel. They with one accord agreed that the question laid before them had been already adjudicated upon with full knowledge of the Apostolic See, and that this renewed discussion and examination of the issue had only served to

---

[48] 'Answer to the Apostolic Letter of Pope Leo XIII On English Ordinations', in *Anglican Orders*, pp. 23-67.

[49] Avery Dulles, *The Survival of Dogma*, New York, 1971, p. 144. Cf. Karl Rahner, 'Non-Infallible Pronouncements', *The Catholic Mind*, December, 1971, pp. 20-29.

bring out more clearly the wisdom and accuracy with which
that decision had been made.' [50]

3. Similarly, Church documents, including the pages of Scripture, often apply the literary form of hyperbole. Magisterial
hyperbole no less than that in Scripture should not be taken
literally. No one today except intransigent fundamentalists expect
faith literally to 'move mountains'. Catholics should recognize
that form and redaction criticism is also required in the appropriation of bulls. Hyperbole is a literary device. The following
passage in *Apostolicae Curae* includes hyperbole.

> 'We decree that these Letters and all things contained
> therein shall not be liable at any time to be impugned or
> objected to by reason of fault or any other defect whatso-
> ever of subreption or obreption or of Our intention, but
> are and always shall be valid and in force, and shall be
> inviolably observed both juridically, and otherwise, by all
> of whatsoever degree and pre-eminence; declaring null and
> void anything which in these matters may have to be
> contrariwise attempted, whether wittingly or unwittingly,
> by any person whatsoever by whatsoever authority or pre-
> text, all things to the contrary notwithstanding.' [51]

Similar hyperbole — not to be taken literally — was used by
Clement XIV in 1773 when 'perpetually' suppressing the Society
of Jesus.

> 'We declare, therefore, that it is perpetually broken up and
> dissolved, and absolutely extinguished alike as to the
> spiritual and as to the temporal, and as to authority whatso-
> ever of the minister-general, of the provincials, of the
> visitors, and of the other superiors of the society.' [52]

4. The bull was framed in the polemical style of its day and,
moreover, reflected the pathology stemming in part from
insufficient evidence which inevitably afflicts the people of God
even in magisterial utterance. In appropriating *Apostolicae Curae*
we should criticize in the light of the gospel all traces of pole-

[50] 'Apostolicae Curae' in *Anglican Orders*, p. 13.
[51] *Ibid.*, p. 15.
[52] Clement XIV, 'Dominus ac Redemptor Noster' in Artaud de
Montor, *The Lives and Times of the Popes*, Washington, 1910, p. 113.

L

mics, social pathology, and arguments based on incomplete
evidence. The document, for example, takes a restricted view of
priesthood based on the teaching of Trent. But Trent's doctrinal
decree had the limited aim of reasserting certain aspects of
priesthood attacked by the reformers. In its debates and preliminary drafts Trent demonstrated its awareness of the importance
of ministry of the word — but it did not emphasize preaching
in its dogmatic decree because preaching was hardly under
reformed attack! [53] In appropriating *Apostolicae Curae* we must
recognize that less was known in 1896 of the Tridentine *Acta*
and context than is known today; and since 1896 another
ecumenical council, Vatican II, brought out the importance of
preaching which is the 'primary duty' of the priest, [54] and which
reaches its climax in the sacramental sacrifice of the altar. We
must, moreover, concede that the most solemn teaching can be
influenced not only by partial ignorance but also by historically
conditioned polemics and pathology. As much as possible all
effects of sinfulness should be left behind in the appropriation
of tradition by a later period. Karl Rahner writes,

> 'One need only ask oneself whether a statement though in
> itself to be qualified as true cannot also be rash and
> presumptuous. Can it not betray the historical perspective
> of a man in such a way that this perspective reveals itself
> as an historically guilty one? Cannot even a truth be
> dangerous, equivocal, seductive, forward — can it not
> manoeuvre a person into a position where he must make
> a decision for which he is not fitted? If such and many
> similar questions which could be asked are not to be
> rejected from the outset, then it becomes clear that even
> within the truth of the Church and of dogmatically correct
> statements it is absolutely possible to speak sinfully, with
> a sinfulness which may be either individual, or of humanity
> in general or of a particular period.' [55]

[53] H. Denis, 'La Theologie du presbyterat de Trente a Vatican II', in
Vatican II Les Pretres Formation Ministere et Vie, eds., J. Frisque
and Y. Congar, Paris, 1968, pp. 194-232.
[54] Decree on the Ministry and Life of Priests, II, 1, p. 538.
[55] Karl Rahner, 'What is a Dogmatic Statement?' in *Theological Investigations*, London, 1966, Vol. V, pp. 45-46. Cf. Gregory Baum,
'Styles of Theological Reflection for the Future', *Theology Today*,
October, 1971, p. 358.

While the thrust of the following passage in *Apostolicae Curae* is true it reflects the polemical tone common to divided Christians in the centuries following the Reformation. Subsequent ages will do well to discard the polemical pathology as they appropriate the bull.

> ' ... the history of that time is sufficiently eloquent as to the animus of the authors of the Ordinal against the Catholic Church, as to the abettors whom they associated with themselves from the heterodox sects, and as to the end they had in view. Being fully cognizant of the necessary connection between faith and worship, between "the law of believing and the law of praying", under a pretext of returning to the primitive form, they corrupted the liturgical order in many ways to suit the errors of the reformers.' [56]

The Anglican Archbishops contemporary with Leo XIII called attention to the polemical tone of *Apostolicae Curae* and albeit with reticence responded in kind. 'Still it is necessary that our answer be cast in a controversial form lest it be said by anyone that we have shrunk from the force of the arguments put forward by the other side.' [57]

5.   A bull does not provide absolute certitude from historical arguments. Historical argumentation alone, especially when it is concerned with the intricacies of human intentions, can give historically probable conclusions. But there remains the possibility of new data and insights. There is, for example, the possibility that new documents may be uncovered which could produce a new problematic, new questions, and a new decision. The following passage of *Apostolicae Curae* is conditioned by nineteenth century historicism and should be interpreted accordingly.

> 'Hence it must be clear to everyone that the controversy lately revived had been already definitely settled by the Apostolic See, and that it is to the insufficient knowledge of these documents that we must perhaps attribute the fact that any Catholic writer should have considered it still an open question.' [58]

---

[56] 'Apostolicae Curae' in *Anglican Orders,* p. 11.
[57] 'Answers to the Apostolic Letter of Pope Leo XIII', *Ibid.,* p. 24.
[58] 'Apostolicae Curae', *Ibid.,* p. 9.

The bull speaks here as if the data then available to the Holy
See was sufficient to settle the question of Anglican Ordinations
forever. It does not say that new historical evidence and insights
are possible and that they could induce a modification in previous traditional teaching. The historical data and arguments
of magisterial pronouncements are themselves historically conditioned. Augustine stated that even universal councils can be
corrected (*emendare*) by subsequent ones when new information
is brought to light.

> 'Even of the Universal Councils, the earlier are often
> corrected by those which follow them, when, by some
> further experience, things are brought to light which were
> before concealed, and that is known which previously lay
> hid.' [59]

6.   To appropriate the positive statements in the bull it is
important to know which opinions the bull rejected. Its positive
teaching on priesthood should be understood within the context
of the tenets held by the English reformers and reflected in their
innovative Ordinal. Piet Schoonenberg observes, 'If a pronouncement is issued against a certain opinion, its positive statements
should be interpreted in the first place as a defence against the
condemned opinion and not as the only possible definition of
the mystery which is being defended.' [60]

In other words the teaching of *Apostolicae Curae* is not the
only possible perspective into the mystery of priesthood.
Leo XIII, proceeding from a narrow and Tridentine perspective,
asked whether Anglican ordinations (at least until 1662) conveyed that priesthood and whether the succession was broken.
Leo XIII did not ask questions being asked about Anglican
Orders and succession today and his *positive* statements do not
exhaust the mystery of priesthood. [61] The teaching therefore
should be appropriated in its restricted, historically conditioned
sense. Newman pointed out that,

---

[59] Augustine, *Writings in Connection with the Donatist Controversy*,
  ed., M. Dods, Edinburgh, 1872, Vol. III, p. 35.
[60] Piet Schoonenberg, 'Some Remarks on the Present Discussion of
  Original Sin', *IDOC*, 28th January, 1967, p. 10.
[61] The 1971 Synod of Bishops, working in different historical circum-

'The Church only speaks when it is necessary to speak;
but hardly has she spoken magisterially some great principle when she sets her theologians to work to explain her
meaning in the concrete by strict interpretation of its
wording, by the illustration of its circumstances, and by
the recognition of exceptions, in order to make it as
tolerable as possible.' [62]

Whenever the state of the evidence changes significantly there
is a new set of 'circumstances' which includes new opinions
and new questions which cannot be resolved by appealing to
old statements delivered in different circumstances. The following
passage illustrates the limited and time-bound circumstances to
which Leo XIII addressed himself. His positive statements
cannot be appealed to as an exhaustive understanding of priesthood nor can his adverse decision about Anglican Orders be
appealed to as an answer to new questions within different
circumstances.

'For some time, however, and in these last years especially,
a controversy has sprung up as to whether the Sacred
Orders conferred according to the Edwardine Ordinal
possessed the nature and effect of a sacrament: those in
favour of the absolute validity or of a doubtful validity,
being not only certain Anglican writers, but some few
Catholics, chiefly non-English.' [63]

---

stances, reflected different perspectives on priesthood. 'Permanent
evangelisation and an ordered sacramental life of the community
naturally require the service of authority and leadership in charity.
Therefore the unity of evangelisation and of the celebration of the
sacraments in the mission of the Church becomes evident. The
separation or the pure juxtaposition of evangelisation and cultic
action would divide the heart of the Church at the expense of the
faith', in 'The Synod Document on Priesthood', in *Priests USA*,
Vol. II, No. 5 (1971), p. 5. Here we observe how different circumstances induce different positive statements on the mystery. Would
it be accurate, therefore, to say the reformers rejected *all* Catholic
priesthood? signified *no* dimension of priesthood in the Ordinal?
intended to convey *no* dimension of priesthood? and were as a result
without *all* priesthood? Catholic teaching since 1896, while not
directed to these specific questions, suggests that the answer in every
case would be negative.

[62] John Henry Newman, *Difficulties of Anglicans*, London, n.d.,
Vol. II, p. 294.

[63] 'Apostolicae Curae', in *Anglican Orders*, p. 2.

Leo XIII was necessarily a man of *that* time — unless we wish
to claim the magisterium enjoys special revelations into future
circumstances and questions — and taught within the context of
'return' to Rome championed by Cardinal Vaughan, Merry del
Val, Cardinal Gasquet and others. He did not consider Anglican
Orders within the context of eucharistic convergence that has
been discovered in the present century. [64] He did not ask questions about Anglican ministry within the inclusivist ecclesiology
sanctioned by Vatican II and which Gregory Baum describes,
'From a restrictive or closed understanding of Church, Catholic
teaching at the Vatican Council has developed to an inclusivist
understanding of Church. The Catholic Church is here presented
as a community with open doors.' [65] For Leo XIII, ecclesiology
was restricted and exclusivist. Salvation was to be sought in the
Roman Catholic Church to which all separated brethren must
return. 'In returning to His one and only fold, they will obtain
the blessings which they seek, and the consequent helps to
salvation of which He has made the Church the dispenser, and,
as it were, the constant guardian and promoter of his Redemption
among the nations.' [66] Since the growth of ecumenical convergence and the event of Vatican II the circumstances have clearly
changed. Leo XIII's negative decision and his positive statements
must be appropriated with the discontinuities of the historical
process always in mind.

7.   The teaching of the bull shows evidence of certain time-
conditioned scientific, theological, historical and philosophical
presuppositions. When St Paul and, later, the Council of Trent
taught about Original Sin they laboured within a framework
of presuppositions; they presumed these presuppositions but
their presuppositions were not the point of their teaching. As
Baum observes, 'Whatever the fathers of a council may have
personally believed about the first man, they had no intention
of saying more about the universal sin in human life than is

[64] Jarry J. McSorley, 'Unprecedented Agreement on the Eucharist',
     The Ecumenist, pp. 89-90.
[65] Gregory Baum, *The Credibility of the Church Today,* N.Y., 1968,
     p. 26.
[66] 'Apostolicae Curae', in *Anglican Orders,* p. 14.

revealed in scripture.' [67] Certain untaught presuppositions are necessary if the magisterium is to convey any teaching at all. Every magisterial utterance, as Karl Rahner notes, 'is embedded in an historical and social fabric, contains different literary forms presupposed those common unreflected elements common to listener and speaker without which there would be no possibility of mutual understanding at all.' [68]

Both the Roman magisterium and many Anglicans of the nineteenth century used terms which reflected 'common unreflected elements common to listener and speaker'. The Archbishops of Canterbury and York were teaching neither the philosophical nor the exegetical presuppositions of contemporary sacramental theology when they responded to Leo XIII: 'And if we follow this method of judging the validity of Sacraments, we must throw doubt upon all of them, except Baptism alone, which seems according to the judgment of the universal Church to have its matter and form ordained by the Lord.' [69]

Similarly, Leo XIII seemed to presuppose a chain or pipe-line theory of succession. But Leo was not teaching this presupposition when he said,

'When in England, shortly after it was rent from the centre of Christian unity, a new rite for conferring Holy Orders was publicly introduced under Edward VI, the true sacrament of Orders as instituted by Christ, lapsed and with it the hierarchical succession.' [70]

And when discussing the 1662 addition 'for the office and work of a priest' Leo may have presupposed but did not teach the chain theory.

'But even if this addition could give to the form its due signification, it was introduced too late, as a century had already lapsed since the adoption of the Edwardine Ordinal,

---

[67] Baum, *The Credibility of the Church Today*, p. 36.

[68] Karl Rahner, 'What is a Dogmatic Statement?' *Theological Investigations*, Vol. V, p. 44.

[69] 'Answers to the Apostolic Letter of Pope Leo XIII' in *Anglican Orders*, p. 32.

[70] 'Apostolicae Curae', *Ibid.*, p. 2.

for, as the hierarchy had become extinct there remained
no power of ordaining.' [71]

8. Official teaching follows the prudential practice of *tutiorism*.
Encyclicals tend to reflect the contemporary *sensus fidelium*.
In 1896 the 'sense' of most Roman Catholics was that Anglican
Orders were not true Orders. Theologians were proposing
openings — but it is not the practice of the magisterium to
endorse advanced theological hypotheses. Newman noticed that
as early as 1842 the Roman theologian Perrone included the
Acts of the Martyrs among the *media traditionis*.

> 'He gives a reason for the force of the testimony of the
> martyrs which belongs quite as fully to the faithful gene-
> rally; viz that as not being theologians, they can only repeat
> that objective truth, which, on the other hand, Fathers
> and theologians do but present subjectively, and thereby
> colour them with their own mental peculiarities.' [72]

The testimony of the faithful in the nineteenth century was for
invalidity. But historians, theologians, and exegetes kept to their
work. Today a growing number of scholars are asking if Anglican
Orders cannot be recognized as 'valid' against a background
of apostolic pluralism of ministries, the convergence of belief
in eucharist and ministry, the possibility of a resurgence of
eucharistic ministry, the importance of recognition by a community of its ministers, the inclusivist ecclesiology of Vatican II,
and the awareness that 'valid-invalid' approximates 'proven-
unproven'. Among the faithful a manifest yearning for intercommunion is a sign that they too have advanced beyond the
exclusivist ecclesiology of the nineteenth century and would
probably accept a magisterial acknowledgment of Anglican
Orders.

In other words proposals for recognition being put forward
by theologians are under consideration by Roman Catholics. The
faithful, it seems, are prepared to accept *official* teaching
whereby what are today theological proposals become 'safe'

---

[71] *Ibid.*, p. 10.
[72] John Henry Newman, *On Consulting the Faithful in Matters of
Doctrine*, N.Y., 1961, p. 102.

agenda and *credenda* put forward by the Roman magisterium. Rahner writes,

> 'It may be that, seen from an ecclesiastical-sociological angle, even a true but novel view requires a certain "period of incubation" until people have become used to it and have come to experience in practice and psychologically that it is perfectly reconcilable with the old faith of the Church.' [73]

Apostolicae Curae may be received, interpreted, and appropriated as part of the Church's *memoria Christi* even if new questions about Anglican Orders result in new decisions. The future function of *Apostolicae Curae* will be different than its function today. But this bull along with a future declaration of 'validity' by the Pope will together remain part of the Christian heritage.

---

[73] Karl Rahner, 'Exegesis and Dogmatic Theology', in *Theological Investigations*, Vol. V, p. 89.

SUPPLEMENTARY BIBLIOGRAPHY

Barrett, C.K., *The Signs of an Apostle*, London, 1970.

Bourke, Myles, 'Reflections on Church Order in the New Testament', *The Catholic Biblical Quarterly*, Vol. XXX (1968), pp. 493-511.

Brown, R.E., *Priest and Bishop*, N.Y. 1970, pp. 82-86.

Clark, Alan, ed., *Agreement on the Eucharist, The Windsor Statement of the Anglican/Roman Catholic International Commission, December 31, 1971*, London, 1972.

— *Ministry and Ordination*, London, 1973.

Coventry, John, 'Anglican Orders, Reassessing The Debate', *New Blackfriars*, Vol. 52, 1970, pp. 37-41.

Cuming, G.J., *A History of Anglican Liturgies*, Glasgow, 1969.

Dulles, Avery, *The Survival of Dogma*, N.Y., 1971.

Echlin, Edward P., *The Priest as Preacher, Past and Future*, Cork/South Bend, 1973.

— *The Deacon in the Church*, Staten Island, 1971.

Greenslade, L.S., 'Scripture and Other Doctrinal Norms in Early Theories of Ministry', *The Journal of Theological Studies*, Vol. XLIV, 1943, pp. 162-177.

Grelot, P., *Le Ministere de le Nouvelle Alliance*, Paris, 1967.

Lash, Nicholas, *Change in Focus*, London, 1973.

McDonnell, Kilian, 'Ways of Validating Ministry', *Journal of Ecumenical Studies*, Vol. 7, 1970, pp. 244-254.

Modern Eucharistic Agreement, London, 1973 (SPCK pamphlet).

Porter, H.B., ed., *Ordination Prayers of the Ancient Western Church*, London, 1967.

Power, David N., *Ministers of Christ and His Church*, London, 1979.

Rahner, Karl, 'Non-Infallible Pronouncements', *The Catholic Mind*, December, 1971, pp. 20-29.

Ryan, H.J. and Wright, J.R., eds., *Episcopalians and Roman Catholics, Can They Ever Get Together*, Danville, 1972.

Schnackenberg, R., *The Church in the New Testament*, N.Y., 1965.

Tavard, George H., 'The Function of the Minister in the Eucharist: An Ecumenical Approach', *The Journal of Ecumenical Studies*, Vol. IV (1967), pp. 629-649.

173

— 'Roman Catholic Theology and Recognition of Ministry', *Journal of Ecumenical Studies*, Vol. VI, 1968, pp. 623-628.

Tillard, Jean-Marie, *What Priesthood has the Ministry?*, Bramcote, 1973 (Grove Pamphlet).

— 'Roman Catholics and Anglicans: The Eucharist', *One in Christ*, Vol. IX, 1972, pp. 175-191.

Villain, Maurice, 'Can There Be Apostolic Succession Outside The Chain of Imposition of Hands?', *Concilium*, Vol. XXXIV, 1968, pp. 87-104.